YAQUI MYTHS and LEGENDS

YAQUI MYTHS and LEGENDS

COLLECTED BY
RUTH WARNER GIDDINGS

Edited by Harry Behn

Illustrated by Laurie Cook

The University of Arizona Press
Tucson

The University of Arizona Press
© 1959 The Arizona Board of Regents
All rights reserved
Originally issued as Anthropological Paper No. 2

Library of Congress No. 60-63129
ISBN 978-0-8165-0467-1

Manufactured in the United States of America on acid-free,
archival-quality paper.

Contents

Introduction

NO THOROUGH collection or study has been made of the folk traditions of the Yaquis. Only about a score of Yaqui stories are to be found in published form. Alfonso Fabila has printed five stories and three songs (Fabila 1940: 202-205, 212-243). Spicer reviews a half-dozen stories and notes the existence of animal tales among the Yaquis of Arizona (Spicer 1940b: 197, 240-241, 254, 261-262). Beals has published a few Yaqui traditions about serpents (Beals 1933: 78-81) and thirteen myths and tales identified as Cahita (Beals 1945: 215-224). A brief resume of Yaqui tradition by one of their leaders has been printed in an appendix to a work by Holden, *et al* (1936: 216-231). In manuscript form, Johnson has recorded the Spanish and Yaqui texts of a small, well rounded collection of stories (Johnson 1940) and Wilder has contributed a collection and study of the Yaqui deer-songs from Pascua village, Arizona (Wilder 1940).

It is known that Yaqui society has been influenced strongly by Spanish and Mexican culture, judging from indications in historical records and from studies of the modern Yaquis.

In making this collection of stories it was the objective to illustrate two things: (1) the nature of the folk literature of the Yaquis and (2) the influences which successive foreign contacts have exerted upon Yaqui folklore.

Collections were made in Potam, Sonora from February through April of 1942 and during regular visits to Pascua and Barrio Libre near Tucson, Arizona from May to September of the same year. The notes on the narrators refer to this period.

Cultural Setting

Language

THE YAQUIS are a Sonoran tribe. They are Cahitan-speaking peoples, affiliated linguistically with the Tarahumaras, Opatas, Conchos, Mayos, and other nearby tribes. Aboriginally, the Yaquis and the Mayos occupied the flood plain areas from the town of Sinaloa north to the pueblo of Cumuripa on the Yaqui River in Sonora (Sauer 1934: 79). Cahitans are of the Uto-Aztecan stock. Of the tribes which adjoined the Cahitan territory to the north, only the Hokan-speaking Seris were not Uto-Aztecans. On the east, the Cahitans were bordered by the Sonoran tribes of the foothills. These tribes separated the lowland Cahitans from the Tarahumaras of the plateau who were also of Uto-Aztecan stock. On the south, the Cahitan area was bordered by rude, barranca or coastal tribes such as the Guasave. These were possibly variants, culturally and linguistically, of the Cahitans. No equal number of people spoke a single language in northern Mexico (Sauer 1934: 22-28).

Brief History

YAQUIS have been in close contact with European culture since the Spanish conquest of their region by Jesuit missionaries in 1617. The Spaniards influenced Yaqui religion through the work of the Jesuits, but they also instigated changes in the material culture and social organization of the natives. The Indians were gathered from scattered *rancherías* into eight large pueblos, each with its church at the center. Governors were appointed by the Spanish and new forms of civil rule were introduced. For the Yaquis, the period of Jesuit occupation was one of peaceful acculturation and material development.

In 1767 the Jesuits were expelled from the region. Foreigners exploiting the riches of the area brought the Yaquis to a state of unrest. The new Mexican government attempted to tax the Yaqui land. In 1825, Juan Banderas began a united Indian revolt against the Mexican inhabitants of the Yaqui region (Troncoso 1905: 112). For six years fighting continued intermittently and the Yaquis learned the use of fire-arms. Temporarily they drove out the Mexican settlers.

These early victories of the Yaquis can be attributed to the weakness of the politically disunited Mexican government. As Mexican internal unity was re-established, war without quarter ensued. This was the beginning of a century of intermittent strife between Mexicans and Yaquis.

In 1876, the great Yaqui leader, Cajeme, took advantage of Mexican disunity in Sonora to drive again the Mexican settlers from the Yaqui valley. When Cajeme was executed by the Mexicans in 1887, another Indian leader, Juan Maldonado Tetabiate, continued the revolt of his people. As the strength of the Mexican army increased, Yaquis were forced either into guerrilla bands in the rugged mountains of the region or into hiding as laborers on Mexican ranches, in mines, or on the new railroad which was being built. Indians in hiding secretly sent supplies to their troops in the hills, and the raiding continued.

In the early 1900's Governor Yzábal of Sonora inaugurated a policy of deportation against the Yaquis. Captives were sent to Yucatan to work on henequen plantations. Many executions took place (Calvo 1949: 96). Peaceful Indians suspected of helping the raiders were hunted out. Many were killed and families were separated. This caused a great reduction in the numbers and efficiency of forces in the mountains, since their source of ammunition was cut off. Mexican settlers filtered back into the Yaqui valley under protection of Mexican troops (Spicer 1943a: 23).

However, small bands of Yaquis still fought on until as late as 1927. Thus, for forty years Yaqui culture was forced into dormancy. A few Indians were living in the hills and many more were living

7

and working with Mexicans and so were subjected to various foreign influences. Since 1927 some nine thousand Yaquis have returned to their region, repopulating many of their old pueblos and following the old way of life.

In 1937 the Mexican government's attitude changed toward the Indians. President Cardenas set aside for the Yaquis twenty per cent of their original territory (Fabila 1940: 194). Here they live today under Mexican military supervision, although they govern themselves in most ways.

Since the late 1920's the official Mexican policy has been more friendly and constructive, aimed toward educating the natives, improving their material welfare and attempting to break down past social barriers between Indians and the Mexicans. However, social barriers in the region are still very real. Slowly, the new policy of contact is inaugurating a period of acculturation for the Yaquis along lines of directed change. There has been and promises to be little decay in the traditional ceremonial life of the Yaquis which has survived the period of persecution and forms the backbone of Yaqui culture as it is being practiced today (Spicer 1943a: 28).

Environment

THE FEELING among Yaquis, wherever they may be, is that the true center of their culture is in the eight pueblos which cluster about the mouth of the Rio Yaqui in Sonora, Mexico. In recent years, five of the eight pueblos have suffered varying degrees of depopulation. The nine thousand or so Yaquis in their valley today live mainly in the Pueblos of Potam, Vicam and Torim. Various small rancherías are scattered along the river. Some Indians live in all of the traditional eight pueblos except one, Belen, which is deserted because of a complete lack of water in its vicinity.

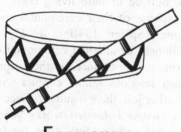

Economy

THE YAQUIS are agricultural. Twice each year floods make the rich, alluvial land along the river ideal for crop raising. In order to farm, the river bottom is first cleared of a dense covering of underbrush, such as *tuna* and *pitahaya,* native bamboo, willow, large mesquite trees and cotton-wood trees. The aboriginal crops of corn, beans, and squash are supplemented by foods introduced by the Spaniards and Mexicans. Wheat is grown in quantities enough for export. Cattle, horses,

9

mules, goats, pigs, and chickens are now an added source of livelihood (Fabila 1940: 8-33). Some wild foods are gathered from the wilderness (called *monte* by the natives), such as honey, wild greens, and tubers. Snares are set for small animals. Larger game abounds in the foothills, and fish are caught in the Gulf of California.

Nearly all Yaquis live from the land, although the making and selling of bamboo mats, willow baskets, or wheel-made pottery supplements the economy. Also an important item in the support of nearly every Sonoran Yaqui family today is the wages paid every two weeks to most Yaqui men, as soldiers (Spicer, E. H. and R. B. 1942). This approximates a form of dole.

The greatest economic drain upon Yaqui families, outside of bare living costs, appears to be the expense of their ceremonial and religious obligations (Spicer 1940b: 44-47, 236-237). The fulfillment of all such ceremonial obligations is of primary importance to the community. In fact, when religious affairs conflict with farming or some other job, the job suffers. Since the church governor *(teopo kobanao)* works year round at official duties and has little time for farming, he is often supported by the people of the pueblo.

No great extremes exist in regard to wealth, although some are better off than others.

The Past

ACCORDING TO what has been reported of Yaqui culture in early times, they were an agricultural food-gathering and hunting group, living in rancherías scattered along the lower reaches of the Yaqui River. They used a wooden mortar in preparation of foods, hunted with bow and arrow (sometimes poisoned), clubs, and perhaps spears. A carrying yoke was employed, as it is today. Their clothes were made of skins. Tattooing and nose and ear-piercing were practiced. They lived in small, scattered clusters of houses, until the missionaries brought them into eight larger communities, each centering about a church. Their homes no doubt resembled the spacious, rectangular units with adjoining ramadas in which the Yaquis live today.

Social and
Ceremonial Patterns

SPANISH INFLUENCE brought a greater development of agriculture and a gradual change to European modes of dress. During the last century the Yaquis adopted the use of fire-arms. The bow is now used only ceremonially and in hunting, sometimes by children. Lately, some modern mechanical devices have been adopted in the household, and a few machines are used in the fields. Some native craft work is still made by both men and women. Foreign crafts such as wheel-turned pottery and machine sewing are usual.

TODAY, the Yaqui social and religious patterns are strongly reflective of the Spanish culture which was imposed from the seventeenth into the nineteenth centuries. The Yaqui military organization, god-parent system, and much Catholic tradition and ritual were adopted from the Spaniards and merged with aboriginal practices to give a distinctive cast to what, by the late 1800's, was a well-integrated culture. Yaqui society is different from that of the Mexicans of the region not only because of its aboriginal aspects but also because it has retained antiquated traits of seventeenth century Spanish culture.

In Sonora the Yaquis still govern themselves in the old way. Matters of importance to the pueblo are discussed at a village meeting or council, called a *junta*. This is attended by the five governors *(kobanaom),* the ex-governors, or elders *(pueblo yo'owe),* the military society *(sontaom),* and the church officials and members of ceremonial societies. This body of civil, military, and religious leaders discusses and decides all matters. Cases involving people from different pueblos are treated by a joint junta of the pueblos concerned. Ritual and praying accompany the discussion at these gatherings. The opinion of the elders is respected. A Yaqui culprit's punishment may be measured in the lashes of the rawhide whip carried about the waist of an official called the *alawasin*. The stocks, also an early Spanish method of punishment, are known to the Yaquis.

The oldest man or woman in the household is considered its head. Often three generations dwell together in a household, which is the basic unit of Yaqui society. There is no apparent rule stating whether a newly married couple should live with the boy's or the girl's parents. The god-parent relationships, sanctioned by the church, are an important part of the social structure. These supplement the primary kinship circle and are a stabilizing factor in the community. These relationships have been enlarged and specialized by the Yaquis and provide each person with a wide circle of ceremonial kin with mutual obligations.

Little is known, from record, of the social and religious life of the Yaquis before Spanish contact. It is difficult, today, to determine which of their cultural practices are aboriginal survivals. Spicer suggests similarity between aboriginal Yaqui social and religious organization and that of the more advanced Pueblo groups of the Southwest. According to him, survivals in Yaqui culture indicate the "possibility of patrilineal clan (gens) groups, an important system of ceremonial societies somewhat similar to those of the Pueblos, and an elaborate ceremonial calendar and ritual"

(Spicer 1940a: 22). The Yaquis' early kinship system, which is being partly replaced by the Mexican system, is considered Yuman in type. The relative age distinctions, evident in kinship terminology, are still remembered in terms employed for members of the elementary family. Although Yaqui interpretations of Catholic ritual surround birth, marriage, and death, often symbols of the earlier ceremonialism accompany them. The formal structure of aboriginal ceremony has disintegrated, but fragments of it remain interlaced with the new Catholicized religious organization.

Since Jesuit times, Yaqui community life has centered about the church. All village officials, civil and military as well as religious, have duties in the church. Both religious and social activities are centered about the events of the Catholic calendar and the performance of the ceremonies attending birth, confirmation, marriage and death (Spicer 1940b: 104-236, 95-116). These rites and ceremonies take place both in the church and the household.

Yaqui Story Telling

STORY TELLING among the Yaquis today is quite informal. There appears to be no socially determined time or place for relating the myths or tales except in the case of *pascola* stories, which are told at fiestas. Nor are there special persons who are supposed to tell the myths or tales. Yaquis say that stories are most often told, by men or women, in the evenings when a group happens to be gathered in the ramada or in the house by the fire. They also tell stories when working in the fields. Some of the older Yaquis indicate that story-telling used to be more formalized in the time of their parents or in their own youth. They also believe that the folk literature as a whole was more familiar to all Yaquis in earlier times than it is today. Most of the Indians today know some myths and tales but no one person was encountered who knows all of the stories in this collection. The myths or legends and tales which appear to be of pre-Spanish provenience do not seem to be as widely known and, in some cases, appear to be only partially remembered fragments of more complete myth cycles. Even the Jesuit period myths giving origins for Catholicized ceremonies are not by any means familiar to everybody who participates in the ritual. It is a general observation that most Yaquis have slight knowledge of pre-Spanish myths and tales and that a broad knowledge of these is limited to old people, members of conservative families, and persons with special interest in the past or in folk stories. More widely known are the recent myths of warfare, of traditions which support Yaqui claims against Mexican encroachment upon their territory, and tales of the Jesuit and more recent periods, particularly the pascola stories.

The subject matter of myths or legends and tales, the traditional themes, characters, and beliefs, reflect a society which has been in contact with foreigners for three centuries. Although many stories show considerable foreign influence, they are usually given a Yaqui background familiar to the narrator. The style of wording appears to be more individual than formal. However, different narrators are often consistent about the sequence of events. Formal endings are not always used. Kinship and occupations of characters are frequently mentioned. Names are usually given. Geography is often related to the action of a story. Since these characteristics seldom occur in tales of foreign introduction, and since they are usual in the earliest type of myths and tales, most often told in the Yaqui language, this may indicate that such traits are remnants of a formal style of storytelling employed more commonly in the past.

The characters in early Yaqui stories are not elaborately drawn. They represent the common Yaqui social personality, conception of supernaturals, and the animals. New characters entered folk traditions as the Indians became familiar with Bible traditions, European history and folk stories. Eventually the Catholic pantheon merged with and partly submerged the aboriginal one; Spaniards, Moors, and the Devil joined Yaqui historical characters, and rogues, adventure-seekers, and kings of European folklore became a part of Yaqui folk traditions. The characterization of heroes reflects changing standards from early times to the present. For instance, heroes of early tales are often obedient, wise, powerful, and great leaders or hunters. In Jesuit-period myths and tales, they become pious or sinful, according to Yaqui-Catholic standards. More recent stories feature pranksters, merchants, warriors, or cowboys.

Subject matter may be drawn from traditional and modern tribal belief. Plots are generally simple, consisting of one or two related incidents.

The pascola story-teller is undoubtedly an aboriginal Yaqui institution. Today, he is only superficially allied with the Yaqui-Catholic religion through appearing at religious fiestas, at children's funerals, and as a dancer on the morning of Holy Saturday. His stories suggest that they are of an early kind which have changed only as the society about which they are told has changed.

Yaqui attitudes regarding their folk literature vary. Older persons in the group learned to know and respect ancient belief during their youth, from elders and from group influence, before the people were scattered during the Mexican persecution in the early 1900's. Such older persons

17

and members of conservative families, often those who remained hidden in the mountains throughout this period, are better acquainted with ancient tribal traditions and value them more highly. All Yaquis associate their folk literature not only with entertainment but also with pride in their history and culture.

Primarily, myths and legends are considered entertaining history and the tales as pure entertainment. As a body, the folklore is not considered sacred, although it is associated with native religion and ritual. Some stories are of social importance because they point a moral.

Much of the history claimed by the Yaquis has been borrowed, but they consider it their own and do not distinguish between history and tradition. Recent stories about warfare with the Mexicans demonstrate the bravery of Yaqui warriors and the justice of their cause. Earlier legends concerning warfare are told today as expressions of their feelings about the cruelty or treachery of the Mexicans, or the superiority of the Yaquis.

Many legends reflect the Yaqui feeling that their region is rightfully theirs. Tales of ancient heroes or saints defining Yaqui territory in mythical times are told as proof that the tribe is justified in defending its land. Ancient myths are set in specific parts of the Yaqui region, giving significance to the spot where the talking tree stood, the pueblo where Jesucristo was crucified, or the waterhole to which a priest condemned an evil monster to live. The origin of the names of hills is described. The spirits of their ancestors, the Surem, are said to dwell in the sea, inside

18

of mountains, or in the forms of ants. Other traditions say that serpents or spirits inhabit certain bodies of water, that the rain is an evil one-eyed god, and the shooting star a brave dwarf hunter. Animals are sometimes possessed of magic powers and should be respected. Some animals are described as culture heroes, such as the *toli* who introduced the first pascola drum and flute, or the badger who named the sun. The deer is able to make himself invisible, and snakes take on human form. The numbers three and four are magical. A special kind of wood in a bow or an arrow enables a hero to perform great deeds. The smoking of native tobacco inspires the power of prophecy. Witches have the ability to take animal forms. Such magical beliefs may appear in stories from any period, even the present.

Myth cycles about nature deities, animals, and magic were undoubtedly a part of Yaqui religious practice prior to their contact with the Jesuits. However, today, any sacred meaning in them has been transferred to the saints and Catholicized ceremony. Old Yaquis or members of conservative families still hold to many pre-Christian beliefs about the supernatural, but such beliefs are considered secular rather than sacred truths. There is no worship of nature deities. Evidently children today are not taught such beliefs, for they know little about personifications of the elements or the powers of the animals.

In a few cases nature deities can be identified with Catholic concepts. For instance, Yuku is often called the Devil, and Suawaka is sometimes called San Miguel. This may indicate an effort to rationalize the existence of both sacred and secular deities.

Yaqui moral standards, implanted by the Jesuits, are given sanction in certain tales. For example: heroes are often described as obedient or pious. Leaving a wife or having sexual relations with a person who stands in the *compadre* relationship promises dire results. Drunkenness, disobedience to one's elders, traffic with things of the Devil, or murder lead to an evil end.

The Yaquis feel that fiestas are both a means of worship and a kind of entertainment. The junta, or political gathering, is an element in so many stories that it may well have been the means by which Yaquis of the eight pueblos governed themselves since earliest times.

Yaqui social attitudes are reflected in stories derived from foreign sources. Even biblical figures become Indian in character in the retelling of familiar Christian lore.

In conclusion, Yaqui folk literature expresses the tribe's sense of superiority, the sacred and material value of their territory, and the antiquity and distinctiveness of their customs.

The Narrators

Ambrosio A. Castro

Age, 54. Born in La Palma, Sonora, and lived there or near Cocorit most of his early life. His father was from Cocorit and his mother from Bacum. During his youth he lived with his paternal grandmother, a curer or "good witch." From her, he learned many ancient beliefs and tales. His great-grandfather was said to have been a very famous *pascola*. Castro has many relatives and friends in the Yaqui pueblos and enjoys visiting about. At present he has no ceremonial affiliations. He fought under Generals Matus and Espinosa with the conservative Yaqui faction, but, later, when Yaquis were being hunted out and deported, he lived like a Mexican, away from the Rio Yaqui. He worked as a house man, a muleteer, railroad worker in Guaymas, and, much later, as a candy vendor and a handyman at the government agricultural school near Vicam. Now, when not farming with his family, he works as a traveling tinsmith, visiting from pueblo to pueblo. He is an extrovert type, mixes easily with all Yaquis, both conservative and liberal; however, some of the more conservative Yaquis mistrust him. He enjoys telling tales and composing poems in both Yaqui and Spanish, although he prefers to use Yaqui for this purpose. He has a special interest in the old Yaqui culture and has a remarkable memory for details. He refused to give detailed information on the geography of the Rio Yaqui for fear that it might fall into the hands of enemies of the Yaquis. He reads and writes both Spanish and Yaqui, having learned to do so when he was past twenty years of age. His information is reliable and of a wide variety.

Lucas Chavez

Age, over 60. Born in the Rio Yaqui region at Torim. Suffered considerably in his youth during the Mexican persecution of the Yaquis, lost his family, escaped to work on a ranch in northern Sonora, then worked his way up into Arizona on the railroad. Has since lived in Pascua, near Tucson, Arizona. Has a good memory for details of ancient lore which he heard in his youth. Can read and write Spanish, took part in the establishment of the village of Pascua. In Sonora he began his training as a *temasti* in the Yaqui church at Torim. In Pascua, he has acted as third *maestro* or *temasti*. Lately he has been influenced by Baptist missionaries in Pascua. His attitudes are bitterly anti-Mexican and pro-American. He speaks both Yaqui and Spanish. His information reflects a good knowledge of Yaqui-Catholic ritual and of Yaqui customs and mythology.

Rafael Lopez

Age, about 45. Born in the United States and lives in the Yaqui colony, Barrio Libre, near Tucson. He has no ceremonial affiliations or ceremonial kin. He remembers little of his native culture and hardly speaks any Yaqui. One of his sons is married to a Papago girl. His attitudes toward Mexicans and Americans are equally favorable. His home life resembles that of the Mexicans. He can read Spanish. As an informant, his value lies in the fact that he exemplifies the marginal type who has moved away from his culture, though he still thinks of himself as a Yaqui.

Mariano Tapia

Age, about 55. Born and lived in the region of the Rio Yaqui until the age of 15 when he was captured and put to work on a Mexican fishing barge out of Guaymas. Later, he came to Arizona where he has worked on the railroad and as an adobe-layer and plasterer, living in the village of Pascua. His wife and children are active members of the Baptist church in Pascua. His attitudes toward the Mexicans are unfavorable. He desires, but fears to return to his homeland. He regrets that his children show little interest in the ancient Yaqui tradition.

23

Juan Valenzuela

Age, about 55. Native of the pueblo of Rahum. He heads the *pueblo-mayor* group of Rahum, and is an ex-governor. He and his family took active part in wars against the Mexicans. They lived in the sierras when they were driven from their pueblo. He is now an active leader in the most conservative faction of Yaquis and one of the chief powers in the movement to re-establish Rahum in the place it had before the revolution. He has worked on the railroad as far north as San Francisco and knows Yaquis in the villages near Tucson, Arizona. Today he supports his family by farming. His attitudes toward Americans are favorable, but cautious. He trusts no Mexican and likewise is distrustful of many Yaquis, who, in his mind, are traitors to the Yaqui cause by compromising with the Mexicans. His knowledge of Yaqui-Catholic ritual is broad. He was the only informant encountered who knew some of the ancient Yaqui traditions by rote. He stipulated that the information he gave should be printed only in English and only in the United States, in order that Mexicans might not read it. He speaks and writes in both Yaqui and Spanish.

Since the greatest number of stories in this collection were told by Ambrosio A. Castro, those not designated as to source are his. Those told by Lucas Chavez, Mariano Tapia, Rafael Lopez, and Juan Valenzuela are marked with the initials LC, MT, RL, and JV.

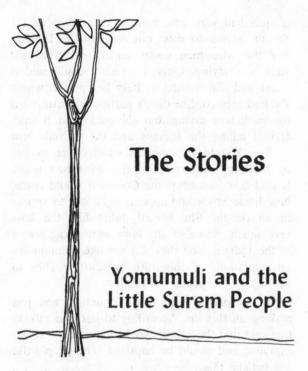

The Stories

Yomumuli and the Little Surem People

LONG BEFORE the Conquest of the Spaniards, when all of the land which is now Mexico was wild, this country was called Suré. It was thus called because it was populated by the Surem, children of Yomumuli. All Indians, the Hueleves, the Opatas, the Pimas, the Papagos, the Seris, were created by her. At that time there were animals living on land and in the water. Huge turtles lived in the permanent water of the river and the sea. This was before we had agriculture.

There was a huge thick stick which reached from the ground to the sky. This stick kept talking, making a humming noise like bees. The

Yaquis had very wise men in those days of the Surem, as we do now, but none of the Indians, nor the wise men could understand what the stick was saying. Only Yomumuli could understand and she wanted to help her people whom she had created. She didn't particularly care what the stick was saying, but she told what it said. It was telling the Indians and the animals how to live. It told the animals which were to live by hunting, and which to live by eating grass. It told how, someday, the Conquest would come, how Jesucristo would appear, as he was to appear to all people. She herself didn't like the laws very much. Some of the laws were disagreeable to the Indians, and they did not like Yomumuli's interpretations of the truth as sent by Dios in the sky to the people on earth.

Many people said that Yomumuli was just making all this up. According to her, the talking tree said that the people would soon have leaders, captains, and would be baptized. The people did not believe this.

Yomumuli was angry that her people did not believe, though she herself felt as they did. It didn't matter to her what this stick was saying. She did not like it. But she knew that it was true.

Since she did not like what was going to come to pass Yomumuli decided to go away. She was angry and decided to take her river with her. "I am going north," she said. And she took this river, rolled it up, put it under her arm, and walked away on the clouds toward the north.

The people did not like the prospect of this Conquest which was coming. So they either descended into the earth to live inside of hills or they went to live in the sea. They were very powerful people, these Surem. Yomumuli left a chief on each hill and the hills were named for these men. These chiefs did not like the coming Conquest either.

Only a few people liked what the stick predicted and these waited. These men are the Yaquis. They grew to be taller than the Surem who had gone away. The Surem were little people, but very strong. They still live in the hills and the sea. They favor man and help him when they can. Some, in the sea, are like sirens and live on islands. Others are whales who come near to a boat to warn it when it is in danger. All of the Surem are wild pagans. If a Yaqui is lost in the monte, these little people help him by bringing him food and fire, and then they go away. Some say the Surem are very rich and have many cattle under the hills. LC

The Papago story of the Ashes People mentions a talking tree (Densmore 1929: 23). A myth of the Tepecanos of Mexico resembles the last part of this Yaqui myth in telling of half of the people being opposed to the coming of baptism and going away to the north (Mason 1914: 148-149).

The Ku Bird

AMONG the Yaquis there was once a bird who, from birth, was very poor. So poor was this little one that he had not one single feather on his whole body. Often he sighed, especially in the winter time, because of his lack of protecting feathers. Many years passed, until one day he spoke to the Owl, saying,

"My brother, do me a favor and I will help you as long as I live. Help me to dress myself by lending me just a few of your feathers, even if they should cover only a part of my body. With the cold weather, I suffer."

And the Owl answered him. "Have no worry about my helping you. I am going to ask all the birds to lend you one feather. In that way, you may clothe your whole body."

"You speak well," said the Ku Bird to the Owl. "When I have many feathers, I shall return a feather to each who lent me one."

"Good," said the Owl, "I shall send messengers to all the birds both large and small, to every single bird, in order that not one shall fail to attend the council. By early tomorrow morning we shall all be gathered to consider the matter of your clothes."

"Many, many thanks," answered the Ku Bird.

"Good-by for a while," said the Owl. And he went away to make arrangements with the other birds.

Immediately they all wanted to see Ku Bird. At their petition, although with great shame, he presented himself.

Everyone was very sorry for him. And each bird presented him with one feather. Everyone contributed until Ku's costume was complete.

After thanking them all, Ku said, "To brother Owl I shall return all of the loaned feathers. He will return them to each of you in one year."

A few days later the Ku Bird visited a spring filled with crystal-clear water. Here, many birds with beautiful plumes often came to visit. When the Ku Bird arrived all the birds surrounded him and looked at him in admiration and joy. They believed that he was a prince, and all rendered him homage. They did not recognize him beneath his beautiful, unusual plumage. He looked like a garden of flowers. Some called him the bird of a thousand colors, for he was wonderfully colorful with all his many feathers.

But within a year Ku was lost completely. He was never again seen, although all the birds searched for him, even in distant regions. Never again did he appear.

To this day, the Owl is still hunting for him. He searches and he calls. That is why Owl sings: "Ku, Ku, Ku, Ku," nothing more. He is not able to say Ku Bird, but he can sing "Ku Ku Ku."

Many centuries have passed and no one has ever heard anything about Ku. It is said that he is enchanted, that he now dwells in a waterhole which lies west of Potam near the sea. Yaquis say they have been there and heard him singing.

Ku never paid for his shirt, the Ku Bird, the bird of a thousand colors. So ends the tale.

29

The
Stories

The Wise Deer

THERE ONCE lived a large deer. He was very strong, and very wise. So wise was he that when hunters searched for him, wherever he might hide himself, they could never find him. They might pursue him closely, but he, in his wisdom, would hide wherever he chose. The hunters would pass by, close to him, but never see him.

Thus it went on. There were times when many gathered in a group to hunt him. But he knew when they were surrounding him, and he did not go out from his hiding place. So it was that they could never catch him.

After many years, the deer attained a great age. Then, he wanted the hunters to kill him, for he was tired of living. He presented himself to the hunters. But they would pay no attention to his presence, for they said, "He is now very old."

Many times the poor, old animal followed the trails which hunters frequented in hopes that he might encounter a trap in which he might put his head or his feet, but he could not find them.

In weariness he spoke to the twilight, saying, "Now I render myself up." And he died. The tale is finished here.

Tasi'o Sewa

THERE was once, here in the region of the Yaqui, a native girl who was more beautiful than any other. It is said to this day that there has never been seen such a pretty girl as Tasi'o Sewa.

She married a man called Wi'i Labeleo who made songs, and she had a brother called Beho'ori.

One day the two young men, Wi'i Labeleo and Beho'ori, went out to hunt. But they found no animals, nothing to kill. As they walked along, they came upon a very small ranchería. They robbed some goats and killed all of a family.

They were caught and taken to the nearest *guardia.* There the governors and the leaders sentenced them to death.

Tasi'o Sewa presented herself to the authorities to beg for them. And the Yaquis agreed to set one of them free. They asked her which one she would like to have set free.

Tasi'o Sewa answered, "You may kill my husband. I can find another man, I can get another husband, but I cannot get another brother."

So they hanged the husband and set the brother free. And they named her an intelligent woman.

This is not a tale. It is said to be the truth.

A common custom is to give young women characters a name referring to a flower (sewa). Seataka, Seahamut, Masa'asa'i are the names of flowers.

Yuku

IN THE TIMES when there was no corn, the blackbird told man about this corn that is sown. He knew where corn was and that the Devil had it. Man sent the blackbird up there after it because he knew that this bird was very good at stealing. The blackbird went to the house of Yuku and sat down on a branch, and the Devil said,

"Now what is it that you are going to rob me of today?"

The blackbird did not say.

When the Devil forgot him, the blackbird stole corn and brought it to man, saying, "This is to eat. Make a little hole in the ground and bury it. Take care of the corn while it is growing up."

The corn sprouted but, when it was still little, it was dying of thirst because there had been no rain. Man talked to the blackbird about it and the blackbird said, "I'm going up there to bring rain and then you can irrigate. When the corn has rain it will grow."

"That is well," said man. And the blackbird went to the God of the Rains and said, "You know that man down there, don't you? Will you send him rain?"

"Yes," said Yuku, the God of Rain. "I will go down there right away. You go on ahead of me!" So the blackbird went on, and the god followed him and caught up with him and beat him and threw him about with wind. Then the god returned to his house. So the blackbird returned to man without any rain. He said, "The god beat me with wind. Send someone else to see if he can bring rain."

Then man ordered the road-runner to the house of the God of Rain. The bird arrived at the house of the God of Rain and said, "You know that man down there, don't you? He wants you to send him rain!"

"Ah, yes, good. I'll go there. Hurry up and go ahead of me!" The road-runner had traveled a short distance when Yuku began to throw bolts at him, chasing and beating him with wind. After this, the god returned to his house without reaching the earth. The road-runner went to man and said, "I could not bring rain because Yuku beat me with wind. Now send someone else up there."

"All right," said man, and he spoke with the toad, saying, "Toad, I want you to bring rain to us if you can."

"I can bring it," said the toad. He went up to the house of Yuku, sowing his children behind him on the road all the way. Then he said, "Yuku, you know that man down there, don't you? He wants rain."

"I know," said the God of Rain. "You go on ahead of me and I'll come behind and catch up."

Toad began to return, and in a short time the god caught up with him. Toad was singing along the road and before him on the road all of his sons sang also. Yuku went from one toad to the next and the next and finally arrived where the corn was sown. He irrigated it and it grew. It formed ears, they ripened, and gave corn. Then men had corn.

This myth is included by permission of Jean B. Johnson (1940 MS). In another version of this story, "The First Fire," the toads bring man fire with the help of the crow, the road-runner and the dog. In a third version, "Bobok," the toad brings rain; corn is not mentioned.

The Stories

When Badger Named the Sun

AT THE BEGINNING of the era of the Surem, nobody knew the name of the sun and they wanted a name for it. For this reason they held a council on the bank of the Surem river. Everyone gave his opinion but no name was found for the sun. Every day they studied the matter. They did not know if it were man or woman and so they couldn't decide whether it would be best to give it a male or a female name. The Surem could not agree. They finally invited all the animals of the world to come to a council.

Once they were all present, before the sun came up, at the edge of the river, they made a great group of men and animals. When the sun appeared, a badger came out of a hole where he lived in the ground.

The badger came to the council and said in a strong voice, "The sun being a man, comes out of a hole in the earth as I do." Speaking thus, he ran away.

Everyone ran after him, wishing to pay him honor for his great intelligence. They wanted to give a fiesta for him and to pay him well with abundant food.

But the badger ran away and went into his hole and would not come out. He thought they wanted to punish him. From that time on the badger rarely goes out on the plains. He is still afraid that they might punish him for something.

Two other versions of this incident were encountered. In one, the *tortilla* fish knew the name of the sun; in another it was the rooster who knew. The Huichol Indians have a similar story in which the turkey names the sun (Zingg 1938: 517).

Mochomo

ONCE there was a mochomo, a chieftain of the ants who was driving a mule train of little mochomos. One night it turned very cold and snowed, and the snow killed every one of his train of mules.

"I shall go to the king of the snow," said Mochomo, "He has killed all of my mules!" He went to the house of the king of the snow, saying, "I am angry. Your snow killed my mule train! If you are a brave man you will fight me!"

"Oh, no," said the king of the snow, "I am not brave. I am very soft and weak. There is a man who is stronger than I am and he is the sun. When the sun shines on me I disappear."

"Well, I will go to see the sun then," shouted Mochomo. And he strode off. To the sun he said, "The snow has killed all my train of mules. You are braver than the snow, so I am going to fight you, since you are so strong."

"Oh, no," said the sun, "there is one who is stronger than I. That is the clouds. I have no strength when they cover me."

So Mochomo went to the king of the clouds, offering to fight him. The king of the clouds said, "The strongest of all is the wind. It blows me wherever it wills."

"Then I shall have to fight the wind. Where does he live?" asked Mochomo.

"Down there in that blacksmith shop," said the king of the clouds.

Mochomo went down to the blacksmith shop and strode up to the bellows.

"I am very angry. The snow killed all of my mules. Since you are the strongest and bravest, I am going to fight you!" he shouted.

The bellows made no answer. Then suddenly they blew very hard, blowing the angry Mochomo, chief of the ants, far away.

This is a fragment of a European fable variously named "L'Hormiguita," "El Aguila," or "El Zancudo." It has been recorded in other collections of folklore on this continent from New Mexico, Jalisco, and Oaxaca (Boas 1912: 221-222).

The Wax Monkey

IN A CERTAIN part of the Yaqui region lived a farmer who had many watermelons ripe in his field. He noticed that every morning some of his best, his prettiest, and his largest watermelons were missing. Finally he said, "I would like to know who it is that is eating my watermelons."

So he set to work to make a monkey out of wax. When he finished it, he put it in the middle of his field. "Here you will stay," said the old man to the wax monkey. "If some thief comes along, don't let him get away." He planted the wax monkey there and went away to sleep in tranquility.

During the night, Coyote went into the field to eat watermelon. When he saw the wax monkey he said, "Get out of here and leave me alone so I can eat watermelon." Since the monkey didn't answer, Coyote became very angry and said, "If you don't go away I will beat you." The monkey didn't move, so Coyote raised his hand and hit

37

the monkey on his head, and his hand stuck there. This made Coyote even more angry and he said, "If you don't let me go I will hit you in the stomach with my other hand!" And he struck the monkey in the middle with all his might. His hand went right through and stayed stuck in the stomach of the wax monkey.

"Aha!" shouted Coyote, "then I'll kick you!" And he kicked him with one foot, then the other. Both feet stuck. He then beat his head against the wax monkey and his head stuck. Finally he struck him with his tail and it also stuck.

Early in the morning when the farmer came to his field he found every part of Coyote stuck to the wax monkey. He put the thief into a cage and set a large clay olla full of water on the fire. When the water was boiling, he threw it over Coyote and burned off his fur.

It is said that Coyote ran around naked until he died and the buzzards ate him.

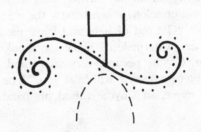

The Stories

The False Beggar

HE WAS FALSE because though he was not poor he asked for alms. Abahta Chaheme was a tall, healthy man but he pretended to be old, dressed as a beggar, and asked for charity.

This man had an only daughter, now grown, whose name was Wokkoi Masa. Abahta Chaheme had many sheep and goats and also horses and cattle; yet he continued asking for alms. He did nothing else. Some people would give him corn. Others would give him two or three little kids or lambs. Thus he had become rich indeed.

Finally one day a young Yaqui man came to his house. This man was a skilled cowboy and a hunter and also a tanner of hides. He made

39

skin clothing and sold it for money. His name was E'esuki. Well, this man fell in love with the young daughter of the rich beggar and she also loved him very much. The young man, E'esuki, talked with the beggar, asking permission to marry his daughter.

Abahta Chaheme said, "Yes, it is well. But to support yourself you must do as I do."

"What is it that you would like me to do?" asked E'esuki.

"Dress yourself as a poor man, use a cane, carry a skin bag about your neck and another over your shoulders and go everywhere, to all of the rancherías and ask alms. This you will do each day until you have fulfilled six months. Then you may marry my daughter."

"Oh, no, sir," said the young man, "I have no need to ask charity for I know how to work at many things. I can earn money in order to support and dress her well and beautifully."

"Then you may not marry my daughter. I will not permit it unless you enter into this bargain."

"But sir," said E'esuki, "I do not know how to ask for alms. I do not want to because I am not hungry. I am an expert hunter. Every day I have fresh meat."

"Well, if you love my daughter and if you want to marry her, beg."

"Thank you very much. Good-by," said the young man, E'esuki.

He went away and in three days returned to the beggar's house to ask Abatha Chaheme again for his daughter. She was a beautiful girl with very large and pretty eyes.

But the beggar did not want to give E'esuki permission to marry his daughter. Then E'esuki said, "Well, father, I will beg for alms for six months because I want very much to marry this pretty little girl."

"Very well," said Abahta Chaheme. And he disguised the boy as a beggar and hung on him two bags and gave him a cane and sent him off.

E'esuki begged for alms and gathered for himself much more money and many more goats and sheep than he had while working at his own trades. He finished the six months and returned to Abatha Chaheme, who said, "Now, indeed, you may marry my daughter. But you must go back to working at your trades."

"But now I do not care to work as I used to. I should like to marry your daughter and continue asking alms in order to support her."

"No," said Abahta Chaheme. "'If you want her, work in order to marry her; if not, don't."

"Well, then, I prefer not to marry. I would rather ask charity even if I could not marry her."

"Then you cannot have my daughter," said Abahta Chaheme.

"I shall not marry then. Good-by." And E'esuki left, and he did not marry. He went on asking for alms, no longer working as a cowboy, or a hunter, or a tanner of hides, but supporting himself as a beggar. He became very rich and died an old man, unmarried.

The girl also never married. No one knows what happened to Abahta Chaheme, but it is believed that he also died.

The Stick That Sang

ON THE RIO YAQUI lived two brothers. They lived with their mother and father. One day they went to some hill, I don't know just where, to pan gold. There were two canyons at this place; one came from the north, and the other from the east. The canyons met there. When it rained, the water brought down gold. The boys went there to find gold. The smaller boy rode a burro and the older one, a mule.

Miguel, the older boy, said, "José, you go up that canyon. I saw a lot of gold up there."

José took his burro and went. Miguel stayed where he was. There was gold there, but in little grains, only as big as wheat.

José hunted up in the canyon for a long time. At last he found a big nugget, a ball of gold. When Miguel came up, he said, "Miguel, I have found a big nugget."

"Let me see it."

"I don't want to show it to you."

"I want to see it," said Miguel.

The two boys fought, and Miguel hit José on the head with a rock and killed him.

Miguel took the ball of gold. He buried José and piled up rocks on the grave. He let José's burro go, and then left.

When he arrived at his home his father said, "Where is José?"

"I lost him," said Miguel.

"Where?" asked the father.

"Over there."

"Well," said the father, "let's go hunt for him."

They set off and encountered the little burro on the road. "Who knows what happened," said the father slowly. He began to cry. Miguel took him to another hill. They found no one.

Many months passed and the muleteers who always went along the road didn't know anything about it. After six months, a straight little stick grew up out of the head of the dead boy. There was a little button on top of the stick.

A muleteer stopped there one day at noon to let his animals graze. He saw the little stick. "How strange," he said, and he grasped it with his hand. Then the stick began to sing, saying, "For a ball of gold, my brother killed me."

The muleteer cut the stick off and carried it with him very carefully.

After traveling three days, he arrived at a pueblo called San Marcial. He took the little stick about the streets shouting, "I carry a stick that sings. Two *reales* to hear it."

"What is this?" said the people. "He carries a stick that knows how to sing? It couldn't be anything. It's not going to sing. Let's see. Let's hear it sing."

The muleteer walked about, holding out his hat. The people threw in money. His hat was almost filled.

Then the muleteer grasped the stick and it sang thus, "For a ball of gold, a ball of gold, my brother killed me."

The people were frightened. "What can this be? His brother killed him for a ball of gold?" Many heard.

Now the muleteer went to another pueblo. He went through the streets calling again, "I carry a little stick that sings all by itself!" Many people gathered. They threw money into his hat. Then he made the stick sing. It always sang, "For a ball of gold, my brother killed me."

Then the muleteer went on to the pueblo of Vicam. Here there were no streets, only one house here, another there, just rancherías. Now the father of José was living there and the muleteer said to him, "Wouldn't you like to hear a little stick sing?"

"Yes," said the old man.

"I will make it sing," said the muleteer. He grasped the stick and it sang, "For a ball of gold, my brother killed me."

"That sounds like my own son!" said the old man. "It sounds like José, the son I lost in the mountains."

Everything was discovered against Miguel. But Miguel said that he did not kill his brother. The father did not know what to believe.

People came from the eight pueblos. And each pueblo had to say one word. Each man who had a thought spoke. And one of them said, "Whoever killed José would be carrying a ball of gold."

And it was found that Miguel was carrying a ball of gold. For that reason he was discovered.

He was stood up in front of six soldiers. They shot him in the chest and he died. They buried him. There it ends. MT

The Two Bears

ONCE IN THE land of the Yaquis there were two very amusing men. One was called Anoki'ichi and the other, Bali'ichi. Anoki'ichi was even funnier than Bali'ichi. The two friends were inseparable. Together, they traveled everywhere.

One day while walking about the countryside they killed a bear. They skinned the bear very carefully, not harming the hide a bit. Anoki'ichi then suggested to Bali'ichi, "Let's arrange this hide so that it is very pretty."

They did. They filled it with grass so that it appeared to be a live bear. That was well. They left it so for a few days. When they removed the grass the stiff hide stood alone looking just like a bear.

Then Anoki'ichi said to Bali'ichi, "Now you get inside of the skin so people will think it is really a bear. We'll go to all the rancherías about here. I'll make a drum and play and sing to you while you dance and act funny. That way we can earn money for food."

This was their plan. Bali'ichi got inside the

45

*The
Stories*

skin and Anoki'ichi put a thick, rawhide rope about his neck. They set off, Anoki'ichi carrying a big stick in one hand and the end of the rope in the other. They visited all the little farms and ranches for many months. Thus, one day they arrived at the house of a very rich man who lived far from any other ranch or pueblo and had a very strong carrizo fence. Anoki'ichi had Bali'ichi dance to a few songs accompanied by his drum. The bear danced, and the owner of the house threw some money out. The bear caught it, gave it to his master, and said thank you by inclining his head and twirling around and around. After the fiesta, the owner of the house decided this bear was very funny and wanted to buy him.

"How much do you want for that bear? I will buy him no matter what he may cost."

"Oh, no, no, sir, I will never sell this animal. He would die of sadness, for I raised him since he was a wee, little one. Why he earns me my living. If you should give me this house full of money, I couldn't sell my bear," said Anoki'ichi.

"Well," said the chief of the house, "then I will give you a cartload of gold for him and you can marry one of my daughters."

"Why, should you give me two cartloads and two women, I should not give you my bear. I hold him in high esteem."

"Then tell me what you would like. The question of the bear's ownership is settled; he is mine," said the householder. And he called two servants and ordered them to get two carts ready and to fill one of them with gold and the other with silver.

"Come on," the rich man said. "You will

have this money and right over there you have a woman. Leave the bear with me."

Anoki'ichi went over to the bear and said, "What do you say, my friend, do I leave you?"

The bear shook his head "no," and wiped his eyes in order that all might see that he was weeping. He stood on his hind legs and embraced his master, Anoki'ichi. Into his ear he whispered, saying, "Don't do this to me. Don't sell me!"

But Anoki'ichi already had his two carts of money and a very pretty girl. Without a bit of shame, he gave the rich man the bear, took the young Yaqui girl and all of the money and marched away. He left poor Bali'ichi, sold.

The bear was put in a big corral where there was another bear. When Bali'ichi saw the other bear lying in the shade of a ramada, he was afraid. This other bear, who was also a man in disguise, was also afraid. He got up and went slowly to meet the recently arrived bear. Each approached the other, frightened to death. They were so afraid as they neared one another, that each was reciting a prayer.

When they got very close together, each heard the other's voice and knew that they both were only human.

"Are you a man too?" asked Bali-ichi.

"Yes," said the other bear.

"Aha. Let's pretend to fight so our master will think we are really animals. Get down like this."

They threw one another about, and struggled for a long time. Then they retired to rest. Thus their master was well satisfied. They fought like this every day, giving each other swats and bites and hugs. For many months this went on.

47

The
Stories

But one day, when the master was sleeping during the siesta hour, the two bears met.

"My face is hot in this skin," said one. "I'm going to take my head off and get a breath of fresh air."

Undoing a string about his neck, he took off his mask and stuck his head out. The other bear did the same, and the two commenced to have a peaceful smoke. They chatted as they sat facing one another.

The owner awoke and saw the two bears chatting and smoking and he realized that they were men. Furious, he went for his bow and arrows. To the bears he said, "Ah, rascals, I found you out today and I am going to kill you both!"

The two bears jumped over the carrizo fence and ran so fast nobody ever caught them. To this day, no one knows where they are.

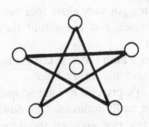

The Walking Stone

THERE was a beautiful young woman by the name of Sawali Wiikit, or, "Little Yellow Bird," who had lovely, long hair, and eyes as shining as a star. But there was one thing about her that was bad. She was disobedient, and she liked to walk about with her friends at night without asking permission of either her father or her mother. She would walk about until dawn and then come home to sleep.

One day, very early in the morning, Sawali Wiikit came into the house to sleep. But before she could lie down her mother spoke to her, "Listen to me, Sawali Wiikit, I don't want you to walk about like this either in the nighttime or in the daytime. I want to you to help me with the things of the household. It would be well for you to stop walking about day and night."

Sawali Wiikit did not reply, but she planned in her heart to continue on her midnight walks in the company of men. She slept, and again at night she left the house. She went to the home of another woman who always went with her. This girl's name was Maso Hubi'aria. She didn't walk about at night, but she would serve Sawali Wiikit pitahaya wine there in her house. That night they drank and became intoxicated. By dawn, Sawali Wiikit was quite drunk on pitahaya wine. When·she arrived home, her mother and her father spoke to her.

Her father said, "If you are not going to stop all of this vice and begin to respect your parents, then you will do me the favor of going away. Go anywhere you please."

"Yes, my father, I will go."

"Wait a moment," he said, and he went out of the house. The young girl waited, and her father soon returned carrying a long, flexible branch. With him came a maestro from the church of Rahum.

The maestro said to the girl, "So you think it better to leave your mother and father forever?"

"Yes," replied Sawali Wiikit.

Then the maestro said to her father, "Punish your daughter so that she will always remember you." So her father gave her three lashes. And he said, "Now you may go."

The maestro accompanied her out of Rahum to the north. Near a mesquite tree he said, "Here you may beg forgiveness of Dios for your sins and your disobedience. If Dios forgives you, you may return to your home."

"But I don't want to return."

"Well, then ask Dios for some penance."

So she knelt and said, "Dios, I do not want to return. I would rather become a tree or a stone or an animal. I do not want to be a good woman."

She had no more than finished speaking when she was changed into a stone.

The maestro went back to Rahum and told what had happened. All of the young people were frightened and were very good to their parents thereafter.

The stone of Sawali Wiikit walked from there to Rahum, to Guamuchil, to Potam, and toward Torim. Sometimes people would put it on top of a mesquite tree, but the next day they would find it somewhere else. Once they found it near Lencho, and they carried it to Torim and put it in front of the church. But it was not there at dawn. It is said that lately it has been seen in the vicinity of Vicam. This is the story of Sawali Wiikit, the walking stone. It ends here.

Sun and Moon

THE SUN loves the moon. She is his sweetheart. He wants her for his wife. But once the moon said to him, "I will marry you, but only on the condition that you give me a gift. Anything suits me, but it must be to my measurement."

"What kind of a gift would you like?" asked the sun.

"It doesn't matter, as long as it fits me."

"Good," said the sun. He brought her a gift, the best that there was. But he could not get the correct measurement. He never could. He would measure her carefully so that it would fit just right. Then he would bring the gift and it would be too small, or maybe too large. So it went on, and he never could fit her.

For this reason, the sun could never marry the moon. He loves her very much and also he wants her because the wealth that she owns is durable. The sun's wealth never lasts. It disappears very quickly. This tale is very sad. LC

Five Friends of Takochai

THERE lived in the land of the Yaqui an Indian called Teta Hiapsi and he was very industrious. He enjoyed building good things. For this reason, he talked one day with a large group of Yaquis to see if they would work for him if he paid them a fair salary. In those days, there were no dollars, or half-dollars. Instead, the Yaquis used for money some silver discs, lacking any stamp, discs about four inches in diameter and an inch thick. They called them *te'okita,* which means pure silver. They also used similar discs of gold which they called *sawai tomi,* which is the same as saying yellow money.

All of the Indians wanted to work with Teta Hiapsi, so he put them to work cutting sticks and branches to make a *serco,* or fence. This *serco* was twenty-four kilometers in circumference and in its center, a little creek ran all the time. In this corral there were lions, bears, tigers, and snakes of many sizes. In fact, Teta Hiapsi's *serco* surrounded an immense forest containing in it a number of water-holes.

Thus Teta Hiapsi considered himself very rich indeed. Also he had a cave, quite wide and deep, full of *te'okita* and *sawai tomi.* From it he paid his workers every Saturday.

One Saturday arrived and he paid all of his workers except one Yaqui whose name was Takochai. To Takochai he said, "You didn't get any money. So you may do anything you want to me to get even." Teta Hiapsi was a very curious man. He enjoyed jokes and pranks, and he knew that Takochai was a clever trickster. He knew that something would happen.

Well, Takochai went away to think of something to do to Teta Hiapsi to get even.

To a little stream which lies west of Cumuripa among some low hills, to a little valley fertile and picturesque, Takochai took his bow and arrows. In this place he met a big Indian. This Indian was so strong that to amuse himself he walked along tearing up mesquite trees by the roots as if they were onions. He would give one jerk and the tree with all its root would come up and he would toss it off into the distance. He did the same with sahuaros. This Yaqui was very strong.

Takochai came up to him and said, "What are you doing?"

"Oh, I'm just pulling up these little sticks," answered the Indian, Hoso Hoseli.

"May I go along with you?" asked Takochai.

"Why yes, it would give me pleasure," said Hoso Hoseli, and the two walked on a little distance together. It was late and they stopped to sleep under a tree.

The next day they took to the road again. They had only traveled a little distance when they met a Yaqui who was pointing an arrow at a mountain range which was so far away that it could hardly be seen.

"What are you doing?" asked Takochai.

"I wanted to kill a deer that was over there in those mountains, but you disturbed me and the deer has gone."

"Oh, but how distant are those mountains!" exclaimed Takochai. "They are barely visible."

"More distant deer have I killed," responded the hunter whose name was Mekkata'obia, which means Light that Illumines the Distance. Takochai invited Mekkata'obia to come along with him and Hoso Hoseli, and the three adventurers went off.

They soon met a tall, thin Indian. He was standing on one foot holding a rope made of hide and tying the other leg which was doubled up. They saluted him and asked, "What are you doing, tying up your leg like that?"

He answered, "I am tying up this leg so I won't walk so fast. With two legs I run as fast as the wind, and with one tied I can walk about as fast as a light breeze." This Yaqui was called Yuku Beo'oti, or Lightning. Takochai and Hoso Hoseli and Mekkata'obia invited Yuku Beo'oti to accompany them, and the four went on together. They went on until it was late and they stopped to sleep.

The next day they again took to the road. After walking only a short distance they met a very short little Yaqui who wore a skin cap. One side of this cap was decorated with red feathers and the other side with green ones. When he put it on with the red feathers to the right the weather became hot, and when he put it on with the green feathers to the right it became cold. He kept making this change every minute, never stopping. This little fellow was called Tasa'a Bali, which means Cool Summer. He is called this because he made heat and cold by moving his headdress of two colors.

The four companions invited Tasa'a Bali to come along with them, and now there were five.

The next day they encountered a man on top of a little hill. He stood with his feet upon a rock and one hand against a tree. With the other hand he stopped up one of his nostrils. Through the other nostril he blew mightily, a volcano of air. The travelers came up to him and asked him what he was doing.

The man on the hill said that over on the other side of the green monte were many Yaquis milling earth and rock to take out the gold. "I make the mills run by blowing with this nostril. There are four mills for the stone and three to draw up water. When I stop blowing, those windmills stop. Right now while I am chatting, they are quiet."

His name was Hekkateni'a.

Takochai and his companions invited this great blower to come along with them.

So the six companions all went on to the *serco* of Teta Hiapsi.

Takochai greeted Teta Hiapsi and said, "I have come to bet with you, Teta Hiapsi, to win from you all that you own."

And Teta Hiaspi agreed to run a race.

Now, Teta Hiapsi had a daughter who was something of a witch woman. It was known that she knew how to fly like a bird. But Takochai was now the chief of five clever men.

Many Indians, men and women and boys, gathered to see the race between the witch and the swiftest of the companions, Yuku Beo'oti. Since Takochai had no money, he put up his life against this witch whose name was Sochik, meaning Bat.

The race was to be from *ili bakam* to *bemela ba'am,* such a great distance that a man on a good horse traveling at a run does not arrive there in one long summer day.

The people gathered and the racers were ready. Someone gave the shout to start. Sochik flew off through the air as fast as she could, and Yuku Beo'oti disappeared like the wind. He soon arrived at *bemela ba'am*, filled his canteen with water and started back. This was the agreement. He who should arrive there and fill his canteen and be the first back in *ili bakam* was to win the race.

When Yuku Beo'oti was about half way back, he lay down to sleep, putting his head on a stump.

Sochik had hardly started for *bemela ba'am*. When she came upon Yuku Beo'oti and saw him sleeping, she threw the water out of his canteen and went on her way toward the waterhole. Then Mekkata'obia, from the great distance saw that the water had been thrown out and he shot an arrow into the tree trunk that served Yuku Beo'oti as a pillow. Yuku Beo'oti awoke and noticed that his water had been thrown out. Taking his canteen, he ran past Sochik to the waterhole, filled it, and returned to *ili bakam* with the water. Thus Yuku Beo'oti won the race and Sochik lost, for she arrived very late.

"I have lost," said Teta Hiapsi pleasantly. And he gave Takochai half of a cave full of silver and gold. "Now, in order for you to win from me all that I own, you and your men must sleep inside of that oven all night."

The oven was big and square. It was used to cook large animals in. There were no windows in it. It was on top of four big flat stones.

Takochai looked at the oven and said, "Very well, we shall all sleep there. And tomorrow you must give me all of your money and your well and your animals."

Takochai and his five companions entered the oven, and Teta Hiapsi, with the help of other Indians, covered it. They put firewood below and above and lit the fire and it burned all night.

When the men inside began to feel the heat, Tasa'a Bali put his cap on with the green side to the right and they felt no more heat.

Dawn came and Teta Hiapsi thought that they must be well cooked. But when he opened the door they all stepped out, alive and shivering from cold.

Thus Teta Hiapsi had to give all of the gold and silver in his cave to Takochai. The companions made a huge purse of many skins. In it they put the money and Hoso Hoseli tossed it up on his shoulders as if it were nothing. He was very strong, Hoso Hoseli, that man who pulls up mesquite trees.

"Now, let us go," said Takochai to his companions. "We will come back for the rest later." And they marched away in triumph.

Teta Hiapsi then gathered together some six hundred Yaquis to follow and kill Takochai and his men. But Mekkata'obia, who could see far, discovered them. The friends stopped at the foot of a little hill above a large plain.

When the Yaquis of Teta Hiapsi came across the plain, Takochai ordered Hekkateni'a, he of the great wind, to blow at them. Hekkateni'a covered one nostril and blew so strongly that the Yaquis were blown high into the air, very high. Then he stopped blowing and the Yaquis fell to the earth like stones. Here ends this tale.

The Man Who
Became a Buzzard

NEAR the pueblo of Bacum there once lived
a Yaqui called Malon Yeka, which means Prairie
Dog Nose. He was a man with deep and profound
desires to know much and have many things
within his power. He wanted to have all sorts of
things, without working. He had a wife and a
number of children. However, he was lazy. He
wanted everything to come to him by miracle.
Also, he possessed a number of strange ideas.
Sometimes he would have the desire to travel
underground, and he dreamed of subterranean
passages which were very dark. Other times
he awoke with the desire to fly like the birds.

One day he took a little cottonwood bench and went off to sit in the shade of a tree near his hut. Seated there with a hand on his right hip, he watched many birds fly about. Among them were some buzzards, vultures, and crows. "Thus, thus I should like to fly," said Malon Yeka.

Suddenly a buzzard came down close to him and said, "What is it that you are thinking about?"

"Almost nothing," answered Malon Yeka. "I was wishing I could be a buzzard like you, and could fly as high as you and see as far as you."

"Well, I am going to give you your wish," said the buzzard, taking off his plumage and wings as if they were a little house. He handed them to the man and said, "Now give me your shirt and pants. We will exchange places for six days. You will become a buzzard so that you may go high against the wind to wherever you desire, and I will stay here in your place.

"It suits me," said Malon Yeka.

"Listen well to me," said the buzzard. "The life of a buzzard is very hard. There are days when there is nothing to eat. Buzzard food is not a sure thing. Sometimes, if there should be some dead animal, you will have plenty. But between times you will suffer much hunger."

Then they parted. The buzzard became a man and the man became a buzzard.

The buzzard, who was now a man, was not accustomed to walking. He went about laboriously, giving little hops because he did not know how to take normal steps like a man. That night he ate the food they served him. Then he went to bed, close to the man's wife. She could not sleep the whole night long because of the buzzard smell. He smelled of dead horse. During the day-time everyone looked with surprise upon his mode of walking.

The man who was now a buzzard did not have any time to fly as he had wished. He hopped about from branch to branch, hoping to find some dead animal. At night he arrived at a ranch where they were making cheese. He was very hungry. He flew down to the house and went close to where they were making cheese. A little girl said, "Look at this clean buzzard! I think he is a pet from some other house. I believe they must have beaten him and he ran over here. Give the poor little one something to eat."

But they would not give him anything.

The man who was a buzzard went away, hop-ping. He was too weak from hunger to fly.

When the six days had passed, the real buz-zard presented himself to the man who gave him back his plumage and his thanks, saying, "I no longer wish to be a buzzard, for I know what hunger is."

Thus they took leave of one another. The bird flew off and the man returned to his house, his desires satisfied. Never again did he wish to be a buzzard.

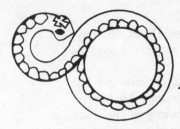

The Snake People

LONG AGO there lived a Yaqui by the name of Habiel Mo'el. He was an orphan, but he had many relatives all over the Yaqui country. This man did not enjoy hunting as most young Yaqui men did. Instead, he liked to travel from house to house and from pueblo to pueblo, attending fiestas and eating and chatting with his friends and relatives.

The only weapon he ever carried was a big, thick club. He lived at the foot of the hill, Mete'etomakame. One day he started out for Hekatakari where there was to be a little fiesta. When he came to Maata'ale, the monte became too thick for passage, and he turned around and went to Jori. From Jori, he cut across toward Bataconsica, where an arroyo empties into the Rio Yaqui. Travel there was very difficult, for the undergrowth was extremely dense. He crawled on his belly under branches, crawled over them, or pushed past them.

When he came upon a sort of clearing, a big snake appeared, crawling across his path. Habiel Mo'el hit the snake right in its middle, but it vanished into the underbrush before he could strike it again. So he continued on his path toward the ranchería at Hekatakari.

Suddenly, what had been nothing but thick monte stretching before him became a large Yaqui pueblo with many people in it, moving about their business. Habiel Mo'el felt very strange. As he walked between the houses, a *cabo* from the *guardia* came up to him, and greeted him.

He told Habiel Mo'el that his chief would like to see him at the guardia. So the two went over there. Inside, on the front bench was seated the head *kobanao*. On the next bench, Haibel Mo'el was told to seat himself. The other *kobanaom* were seated on the other benches. To one side a young girl was sitting. About her waist was a bandage of leaves.

The head *kobanao* spoke to Habiel Mo'el, "We have brought you here to ask you why you beat a girl this afternoon as you were traveling along between Jori and Bataconsica.

Habiel Mo'el was very surprised. He replied that from Jori to this place he had met no one on his journey. "I did not beat any girl," he said.

"You struck a girl this afternoon, and you are liable to punishment. Why did you do this?" insisted the *kobanaom*.

Habiel Mo'el could not remember having done so; and he repeated this. Then he explained where he had come from and his route, saying that he had seen no girl on the path. He respectfully asked their pardon, but insisted that he had done nothing at all.

The head *kobanao* turned to the girl, who was seated to one side, and asked her if this were the man who had beaten her.

"Yes," she answered. "'And he is still carrying the stick with which he beat me and almost killed me. That is the man."

Habiel Mo'el said that he had never seen the girl before and that he remembered nothing of it. He again asked their pardon, but disclaimed guilt. The *kobanaom* considered the matter among themselves.

Then the head *kobanao* said, "We will pardon you this once, since it is your first offense. But after this, when you are traveling, never harm anyone at all who may cross your path offering you no danger. You may go this time."

Habiel Mo'el thanked them and left the guardia. As he went out, he found himself in the middle of the monte with no sign of a village.

He traveled on toward his destination. It was dark when he arrived at Hekatakari and the house of his relative. He greeted the little old man whose name was Wete'epoi.

They sat down to a meal of pitahaya and Habiel Mo'el told Wete'epoi about his strange experience concerning the appearance and disappearance of the large Yaqui pueblo, and of his accusation.

The old man listened and then said, "You have done a great wrong. All animals, as well as people, have their authorities and their laws. You hurt a snake which crossed your path, doing you no harm. The authorities of that group took action against you. You must never again do that thing. The chiefs of the snakes met when the girl complained. They turned into people to punish you. I will give you some advice. Never hurt any snake, coyote, or any kind of animal, which is just crossing your path and offering no harm. If a snake lies coiled in the path, kill it. You are defending yourself then. But always kill it completely, never let it get away or it will complain and its chiefs will punish you."

Omteme

WHEN YOMUMULI took her people, the Surem, and went away to the north because she did not like the things said by the talking stick, she left governors behind for each region. These chiefs lived on the tops of mountains along the Rio Yaqui. There was one governor who lived in the hill of Omteme. He was very wise. He knew that the Conquest would come and all of the things it would bring with it. He knew that it would come with two words—good and bad. All of this he knew from the stick that talked. The name of this chief was Omteme, which means "He is Angry." Omteme was standing on top of his hill when Columbus came into port at Guaymas. He was very angry because he knew that the Spaniards were coming with treachery.

Columbus climbed a hill near Guaymas, which is now called Takalaim and he saw Omteme in the distance. Omteme wanted to know what the conqueror intended to do, so he asked, "On what conditions do you want to make the Conquest?"

Since Columbus did not have a good heart,

he took his big gun and shot at Omteme. The shot fell short and Omteme asked again, "What do you want? What are you doing?"

Columbus shot a second time, this time coming closer, but not quite reaching Omteme. The chief did not understand guns. He still kept asking of the conqueror how he intended to make the Conquest.

Columbus shot a third time and the ball reached the foot of Omteme's hill. When Omteme saw the shot he said, "Oh, so you want war!"

He took his bow and an arrow and he shot. The arrow hit the top of the hill on which the conqueror stood, splitting the mountain in two. The conqueror fell into the sea and drowned.

Then Omteme spoke to his people. "You who wish to, may stay. I am leaving now." And he descended into the heart of his hill.

Most of the people also went into the mountains or into the sea, for they could not accept the Conquest. Like their chief, Omteme, they said, "I am leaving now."   LC

Juan Sin Miedo

JUAN SIN MIEDO was so called because he could not conceive of what it was to be afraid of anything. Once he was asked to be caretaker of a certain house which the owner could not get anyone to stay in overnight. It was said to be full of spirits and ghosts. Juan said that he would stay there, of course.

So Juan went there to live. The first night as he was sitting in one of the rooms he heard a voice from up in the ceiling say, "Shall I fall, or shall I not?"

Juan looked up to see who was talking, but could see nothing. He answered, "Sure, fall if you like."

So into his lap fell a skeleton. Juan Sin Miedo lifted the head and looked at it. "Hmm. A skeleton, without any clothes or skin." He threw it into the corner and walked out into the yard.

There he saw a hammock, the one in which the owner of the house, now dead, used to sleep. "So this is where he used to sleep. I guess I'll sleep here too." He lay down and closed his eyes. A moment later he opened them to see, seated all around him, a group of dead people dressed in mourning and seated about a coffin.

"Oh, a funeral. Poor fellow," he remarked.

67

The corpses were chatting and smoking. Juan asked for a cigarette. When a ghost handed it to him, Juan looked carefully at the man's face. "How strange. You don't have any eyes. How can you see?"

Thus he chatted with them. He noticed that when each man finished smoking his cigarette he put the butt into the mouth of the dead man. So Juan did the same.

In the distance appeared a tall man dressed in black. On seeing him approach, the ghosts whispered to one another, "The owner!" and they all ran away in fear.

The man in black rode up to Juan on a big, black mule. "Good morning, Juan," he said. "Have you been here all night?"

"Yes," said Juan Sin Miedo.

The owner of the property looked at Juan with interest and said, "How would you like to be head of all this property? You are the only man who will stay here at night. They have put soldiers with guns around, but they die of fright from hearing noises at night, and so join the rest of us here."

"I'd be glad to be chief here, if there is wealth for me in the offer," said Juan.

The owner pointed to the hacienda full of rich furnishings. "This will be yours if you will care for it. You may also have my mule and clothes, for I must return to the graveyard now that sunrise is about here."

So Juan took the clothes and the mule. When he rode into the adjoining town, the people thought he was the ghost of the real owner and they ran and hid. So Juan became owner of the whole region as well.

The Boy Who Became a King

THREE BOYS decided to leave their mother and father and go away to work. Their mother made a lunch for each of them and they left. They came to a place where there were some fig trees; here, they ate lunch. At this place the road branched three ways. After lunch, the oldest boy said that he would take the road that went straight ahead. "In one year from now we will meet at this fig tree." The oldest boy cut the tree saying, "When blood comes out of a cut in this tree, it means bad luck; if milk flows, it is good luck."

The oldest boy found good work, and married a fine girl, the daughter of his boss. The next oldest boy married a good girl, and he had good luck. But the youngest encountered very bad luck indeed.

Although the country was full of all kinds of animals, he hunted all day long but found no game for his supper. That night he hunted a place in which he could sleep, and he found a cave. In the cave was a lion. And the lion said to him, "Don't you have any bad luck in your travels about this country?"

"No," said the youngest boy.

The lion then said, "Don't you want to be my captain?"

69

The Stories

"Good," said the boy, "but I don't know how to talk your language very well."

"That is all right," answered the lion. "You'll learn soon." The lion took out a horn, blew it, and called all the animals together. When the animals of all the world were there together, the lion talked with them about making this boy their captain. They all said that they would like him for a captain.

Then the lion taught the boy how to talk with every kind of animal. When the boy had been there a month a crow came to see him, and she said, "Listen, my friend, I have two little crows. I want them to be baptized."

"Very well," said the boy. "Bring them here. I will baptize them." So now the boy had two little crow god-children. The father crow brought to the boy an egg. "Take this egg, compadre," he said, "and whatever you want, ask the egg for it—it doesn't matter what it is, you'll get it."

So the boy took the egg and set out for a big pueblo. He arrived there very late at night. He took the egg out of his pocket and asked it to make him into a negro, and to give him a guitar. In his black attire, carrying the guitar, he stopped at the house of a lady. He greeted her, "Good evening."

"Good evening, young negro," she answered.

"I would like to sleep here," he said.

The lady said, "That's all right." She gave him a supper of tortillas, meat, and beans. When he had eaten, she asked him to play and sing. He did. He knew many songs not known to other singers. The lady was so delighted she wanted to dance.

He slept all night on a mat on the floor. Early in the morning the lady arose. She told him to get up. After breakfast she told him to remain there looking after the house while she went out. This lady knew the king in that pueblo very well.

She went to the king and told him that she had a negro who was very good at playing the guitar and singing.

"Where is he?" asked the king.

"He is in my house." So the king sent a man to bring the negro to him. This man arrived at the house and said to the boy, "The king wants you." The boy was surprised. "Don't be afraid," said the man. "Let's go."

When the king saw the negro and heard him play he was very pleased and said, "What size shoe do you wear?"

"Six," he answered. So the king ordered shoes and a whole set of new clothes made for the negro. Before putting on these new, clean clothes, the negro went to a place where he could bathe himself.

Now, the king had a daughter who was very pretty. This girl wanted to see the negro boy when he had no clothes on, so she looked through a crack at him when he was bathing. The boy had taken off his outer, black skin and she saw him as a very beautiful boy. She said nothing of this to anyone.

After bathing, the boy put on his black skin and his new clothes and went to supper. Afterwards, the king asked him to sing. He took his guitar and played and sang. They all enjoyed it very much. But the daughter knew about him. She said, "That guitar is old. He should have a new one." The king told the negro that he should have a new guitar.

But the boy said, "No, this is just as good as a new one."

A week later the girl told her father that she would like to get married. So her father sent out notices that he who should have one peso more than the king himself would be allowed to marry his daughter. Many rich dukes came and talked to the king, but not one of them had the necessary wealth. The king was always ahead.

When they had all gone away, the little negro went alone to a small hill outside of the pueblo. Here he took out his egg and talked to it. He said he would like to have a palace, better than all the palaces in the world. Before him, inside the hill arose a palace of pure gold. He then asked for it to be furnished completely with tables and chairs of pure gold. And it was. He ordered pigs and horses to be put in the stables and yards. These also were of gold, and they ate golden grains of corn. The boy went out and commanded that a huge iron gate be put across at the entrance. Then he went to visit the lady who had taken him to the king. He did not speak of his palace, but said that he had come to see her. She was pleased and asked him to sing for her.

The next day the negro asked the king, "Why didn't your daughter marry one of those rich men who came here?"

"Because they didn't have any more money than I have," answered the king.

"I have more money than you have," said the negro.

"Where?" asked the king.

"Do you see that hill over there?" The king thought that there must be a rich mine in the hill.

"Yes, I see the hill," said the king. "Let's go see it closer." The girl wanted to go along too, so the king ordered a big coach for her. They came to the hill and the king said, "Where is your money?"

The negro, dismounting, took out a huge iron key. Everyone was surprised as he went to open the gate. They looked in, then covered their faces with their hands because of the brilliance of the treasure inside. But the girl said to her father, "Go in, go in, go in."

They all entered and saw the palace all made of gold. "Look at my pigs," said the boy. They were also of gold.

"You beat me by one pig!" said the king.

"Let's go see my horses," said the negro. The king didn't need more to convince him, but he was always interested in horses, so they went to the stables. The horses were also of gold.

"That's enough. I want to see no more. You can marry my daughter," said the king. The next day the boy married the king's daughter.

The king loved his son-in-law very much. It didn't matter if he was a negro; he was rich. At the wedding everybody danced. The girl danced until she perspired very much. The boy took out a huge handkerchief and wiped her face for her. The next day they went to their palace in the hill.

They were very happy. He talked to her about his two crow god-children. "But," he said, "I must leave you for a while. It is nearly a year since I left home and I must go see my father."

He ordered ten mules loaded down with money and five men to care for them. The girl warned him that he would have to pass a place where there were many thieves. "Take care," she said, "when you pass that place."

"Very well," he replied, and he set out. The next day he arrived where the thieves were. They asked him to stop and play at *barratas* with them. He did, and they won from him all of his mules, with their loads. Next, he lost his fine clothes and had to put on the old clothes of one of the thieves. He sent his five muleteers away, saying there was no more work. Then he set out on foot toward his home.

Since that day had marked a year since he had taken leave of his brothers, he arrived late at the fig tree. He cut the tree, and it indicated good luck by weeping milk. So he went on.

He arrived at his home looking like a vagabond. On seeing him, his parents did not want to admit that he was of their family. His father said to him, "You are no longer my son. Your brothers have done well, but look at you."

That evening they handed him his supper out of the window. They didn't want him in the house. He was told that he could care for the chickens and pigs. If he wanted to stay there, he must sleep in the chicken house.

"Take care that the chickens don't drop on you," said his father.

He went to the chicken house where he was to sleep. When he got there, he talked to the chickens. "If one of you makes a single dropping during the whole night, I'll wring your neck and throw you outside!" he warned them. They all listened attentively.

One chicken said, "This captain is very strict, so be careful."

About midnight, the boy heard a chicken make a dropping. He knew that it was an old, old rooster, but he asked, "Who did that?"

"Not I," said the nearest hen.

"Not I," said the next. And so on down the roost each answered, "Not I." When the question came to the old rooster, he said nothing. The others said that he had done it, and, finally, he admitted it. The boy twisted his neck and threw him outside, a good lesson to the chickens, who did not make a dropping all that night.

The boy's father came the next morning and saw the chicken house clean. "How could this be?" he wondered.

He had some three hundred pigs who were very dangerous and unmanageable. "You are going to take the pigs out today. Be careful, for they are broncos," he said to the boy.

The boy went to the pig sty. There he talked with a big white pig. The pig recognized him as a leader. The boy told this pig to tell the rest of the pigs not to act up that day. And the white pig did so.

The father wanted to count the pigs as they left, so the boy ordered them to pass the gate of the sty in pairs, marching as if in an army. The father was astounded. The pigs marched in pairs out into the country.

The boy said to the white pig, "Tell your companions not to wander far, for I am going to take a nap." They minded him, for they were very contented with their captain. In the afternoon, they returned, marching home to the sty.

The boy thought often of his wife and the

golden palace he had left. In a suit at home he had left the crow's egg. After about a month his wife began to wonder what could have happened to her husband.

One day the boy saw a crow flying overhead. "Stop a minute, compadre," he called to the crow. The crow turned about and came back. It was, indeed, his compadre.

"What happened to you?" asked the crow.

The boy told him all that had passed. "If I had paper and pen, I would write to my wife," he added, for he knew how to write very well.

The white pig had a suggestion. He told the crow to fly out to a trash pile and bring back a piece of paper. Then the pig told the crow to pull out a feather. "Make a little hole in the back of my neck and use my blood for ink."

Thus the boy wrote a letter to his wife telling her where the egg was, and asking her to bring it to him.

The crow took the note and flew to the palace of gold. The girl was seated in the door, sadly thinking. She saw the crow fly low over her and suddenly remembered that her husband had a crow compadre. When the crow said "Crak, crak," she called it to come on down. It turned about and brought her the note.

She went to the suit and found the egg in the pocket. She then ordered ten mules loaded with money. She put on clothes of a man, took her pistol, and set out, accompanied by five men. She arrived at the house of the boy's father, where she was received most graciously, for they thought she was a rich man. At dinner the father of the boy talked of the tramp who was caring for the pigs and chickens. He didn't know quite what kind of a person he was, for the chickens never soiled the floor of their house at night when this man slept there, and the wild pigs were now very tame and marched like soldiers for him.

The woman, who was dressed as a man, watched at the window and saw the boy come for his dinner. As he went to the chicken house, she joined him. She sat with him while he ate. She said nothing of who she was. "If I show you something I have here, perhaps you will remember me," she said and reached in her pocket and pulled out the handkerchief with which he had wiped her face at their wedding. At that, he recognized his wife. She had brought him a suit of fine clothes, and some women's clothes for herself. They were very happy. They spent the night in the chicken house.

The next morning the father complained that it was very late and that tramp had not yet got up to feed the chickens. He went out and knocked at the door. "Get up!" he said. "The chickens are hungry and it is late."

"Excuse me a moment, I'll be out in a little while," the boy answered.

At last he and his wife appeared, dressed in all their finery.

The old man said, "Of course, of course, you are my son."

But the boy, by means of the egg, destroyed his father, the house and everything but the animals. With his wife he went home to their palace of gold in the hill.   RL

Kaiman

DOWN on the Yaqui River the waters of the sea once rose and reached far up into the monte where many things were growing, such as *sinam, choan,* and *ono'em.* Among all these natural plants, the water came and carried with it the great turtle, Kaiman. Thus has it been said.

When the waters receded this great animal remained on the ground among the trees. And it could not raise itself.

After the flood, a Yaqui encoutered this Kaiman stretched in the sun. When the Yaquis see such a thing, they always feel pity. This trait of the Yaquis is very stupid. The man placed the huge Kaiman on his shoulders. It was heavy. And he carried it to the river. Arriving at the bank, he entered the water up to his knees, and started to put the animal down into the water.

Kaiman then spoke, "There is very little water here. Would you be so kind as to carry me out a bit farther. I am very weak and hungry."

So the Yaqui carried him out until the water reached to his waist.

"Oh," said Kaiman, "farther than this, please, just a little farther."

"I can't walk very well," said the man, "but I will do what you ask." Until the water reached his neck, he carried the animal out and then put him down.

"I wish you might have carried me farther out," said Kaiman. "But this will do. Now I would like to ask the favor of eating you."

The man could not move. He said, "Are you not satisfied that I have done you a great favor? Why should you now want to eat me?"

"Don't you know that a good deed is always paid with evil?"

The man was very sad to hear this. He had no strength now. "Very well," he said, "But wait a minute. Over there comes someone who may know if it is right for you to eat me or not."

A dog appeared at the edge of the river to take a drink. The turtle spoke to the dog, saying, "Is it not certain that a good deed is always repaid with evil?"

"Why?" asked the dog.

"Because I should like to eat this man."

"Eat him, then. Man is bad. He beats us."

But the man said, "Wait. Here comes another friend of mine who might help me."

A horse came up. To him Kaiman said, "Is it not true that a good deed is paid with evil?"

"Why?" said the horse.

To him also, Kaiman said, "Because I wish to eat this man."

Said the horse, "Then eat him."

Then along came a goat, and other animals of the household. And every one of them answered, "Eat him."

Last of all came Coyote. Kaiman was getting restless and more and more hungry. But he said to Coyote, "It is true is it not, that a good deed is paid with evil?"

"What's that you say?" asked Coyote. "I am a bit deaf." Coyote had learned this trick from the Mexicans. "Come a little nearer. I can't hear a thing you say."

"Isn't it true that a good deed is paid with evil?" asked Kaiman, moving closer to Coyote. "I want to eat this man."

"What did this man do?" asks Coyote.

"He carried me into the deep water."

"Yes, I carried him here," said the man.

"And from where?" asks Coyote.

"From the monte."

"Well," says Coyote, "Let us go to the monte. There's where the trouble started." Then he asks, "And how did this man carry you?"

"Why, this way."

"Well, carry him that way, then," said Coyote to the man. So the man picked up Kaiman and carried him back to the monte.

"Here we are," says Kaiman.

"Well," says Coyote, "Put him down the way you found him." Then he asks, "Were you in that position?"

"Yes," replies Kaiman, "Like this."

"All right," says Coyote to the man, "leave him there. And don't ever pick up this kind of animal again."

And Coyote ate Kaiman.   LC

The Big Bird

THIS is Yaqui belief.

A great bird lived on the hill of Otam Kawi.
Every morning he would fly out in search of food.
He caught men, women and little children and
carried them back to Otam Kawi to eat. In
those days the people always were watchful. They
couldn't have fiestas because when they had
pascolas, always two or three of the people were
carried away by the big bird. The Yaquis lived
in *hu'ukis,* little houses made of mud and branches
that looked like the house of a pack-rat, because
they were afraid of the great bird.

There was an old man who earned his livelihood by hunting deer. He did nothing else. He
had only one daughter. She was big with a child

who was soon to be born, when the bird carried away her husband. The old hunter, his wife and the daughter only remained, and the daughter pregnant. The baby came in the afternoon.

It was a man child that the girl had. And the old grandfather continued hunting deer.

About a year later the grandmother went out early one morning to bring in water. The bird came by and carried her away. So the grandfather and the girl went on bringing up the child.

The next year the bird carried away the mother, and the grandfather brought the child up on cow's milk. There were cows in those days, but no animals of the claw.

When the little boy was old enough to walk, he went everywhere with his grandfather. He walked all over the monte hunting. This little boy never grew very big. When he was ten, he was still very small.

One afternoon he was seated outside of the house and he said, "I have no mother."

"Ah," said the grandfather, "The big bird carried her away. First he took your father, then your grandmother, then your mother."

"Where is that bird? I am going to grow up and kill that bird."

The old man laughed.

When the boy was older, his grandfather made him a bow and some arrows, and every day he went out practicing. He became very strong. But he was still small. When he was fifteen years old, he measured no more than three and a half feet in stature. He went everywhere with the old deer-hunter, his grandfather.

One day the boy said, "I am going to hunt out

that bird. I am angry." When he was still not full-grown, he went about alone, walking through the monte and looking up into the sky.

There is a level plain east of Potam called *maretabo'oka'apo*. There the little boy walked. He had been hunting for three days. He carried many arrows in his quiver of javelina hide. Then he saw the bird. Quickly he jumped into a hole. The big bird sat down in a mesquite tree, waiting for him to come out of the hole. The boy stayed there all day long, watching the big bird in the mesquite tree. He saw everything; the size, the colors of the feathers, the big eyes, and all. At night he went farther back in the hole and fell asleep. Late at night he awoke. The bird had gone with the coming of night.

Three days later, the boy returned to his home, very late. His grandfather was not there. The boy carried two dark sticks on which he had placed many pitahayas. He hung them near the door where his grandfather would enter. The boy was inside cooking deer meat when the old man returned and saw the pitahayas.

As he entered he asked, "My son, where have you been?"

"Over in the hills."

"Weren't you afraid of the big bird?"

The little boy said, "I saw him. I saw all of his colored feathers and his big eyes. I climbed into a hole. I return only to ask permission to kill the bird. This bow would never kill him. It is too little. I wish you would make me one of that wood called *kunwo*. And I need another kind of arrow, made of *wo'i baka*. I will go as soon as you make me these."

"But you are so little. That bird will kill you," said the old man.

Many Yaquis lived in the neighborhood and they all came over that night to talk. They asked the little boy if he had really seen the big bird.

"Yes, I saw it. It has feathers of many colors, a big body, and long claws. I am going to make a lot of little animals out of that bird."

"This boy is crazy," said an old man. And many of the elders believed that he was. "But we'll see," said these older men. And they went back to their homes.

The old grandfather then made three kinds of pinol. The little boy had asked him to. He made pinol of corn, of wheat, and of garbanzas. When the little boy had this and his bow and arrows, he said, "Call the people together."

All of the people gathered, *kobanaom,* soldiers, women and children. Everybody came, from all of the eight pueblos. They said, "Are you the boy who is going to kill the big bird?"

"Are you the man?" laughed a *kobanao.*

"Yes," said the little boy.

Then an old man who lived near to Otam Kawi spoke. "Wait for this bird near Otam Kawi. He lives there. He only goes away to catch the people. He always comes back there. You will see there a great pile of bones."

The people bade the boy good-by that night, and he said to his grandfather, "Now I know I can kill that bird. I will be back in three days."

Everybody was content. "If you kill him, we can have pascolas again!"

The next day, before dawn, the boy and the grandfather left. At dawn, they saw the bird fly over. But they were safe below the mesquite trees. They walked through the monte toward Otam Kawi. "No farther than this," said the boy, Leave me here. I'm going to find out where the big bird roosts."

All day long the boy waited. At last he saw the bird come in and alight in a large tree. Night fell and the bird went to sleep. Then the boy softly approached the tree. There, he knelt and prayed for a long time. Then he began to measure. He measured twenty-five feet from the foot of the mesquite tree toward the west. There he made a deep hole, ten feet deep. When dawn came, he was still hunting poles and branches with which to cover it.

The bird saw him and was angry. The boy went down into the hole. He prepared his bow well. The bird came down from the mesquite tree and went to the cave. The boy was inside, looking out. He shot the big bird in the eye with an arrow.

The bird flew to the top of the mesquite tree. The boy shot three more arrows. The bird fell.

For a long time the boy did not come out of the cave. He waited to be sure that the bird was dead. When he was sure, he came out and went over to the big dead bird.

He pulled out a handful of its feathers and threw them into the air and the feathers became owls. With another handful of feathers he made smaller owls. With four handfuls of feathers, he made four classes of owls.

In the same way, with other handfuls of feathers, he made birds of every kind, crows and roadrunners. He threw the feathers and they became birds of different colors.

When he had finished all of the feathers, he

cut off a piece of meat from the dead bird. He
threw this and it became a mountain lion. He
cut another piece and made another kind of lion,
which is a little braver. With another he made
the *topol,* and with another, a spotted cat. Thus,
the boy made four classes of big cats. After that
he made four smaller kinds of cats.

With more meat the boy made foxes and
racoons and also four types of coyotes. He made
snakes and all kinds of animals that have claws.

When all of the meat was gone, only bones
remained. He dragged the bones under the mesquite tree and started home. He arrived there
in two days. He came in very happily, dressed
in a suit of feathers he had made from the
bird, and he wore four feathers in his hat, two
on either side.

He entered and his grandfather was frightened
to see him covered with blood from the meat of
the animal.

The old man was afraid, and he said, "What
happened to you?"

"I killed the big bird. Now you may walk
about the world."

The old man rushed out of the house. He
talked with his neighbors who ran to advise those
in other pueblos, and the people of those pueblos
spread the news to others.

People came from all the eight pueblos. They
still walked at night as before, because they didn't
believe the big bird was dead. The governor came,
and when all of the people were gathered the old
men talked. "You really did kill it?" they asked.

"Yes, sirs. I made many little animals out of
the feathers and the meat. I made owls of four
kinds. I made four kinds of coyotes, four kinds

of small cats, four kinds of lions, all animals of the claw."

"Well, let us see if this is true. We will send men from each pueblo, from Potam, from Vicam, from Torim, from Bacum, from Cocorit, Rajum, Juirivis and Belen to see the proof."

"The bones are there," said the little boy. "If they aren't you may cut my neck." And he led off on horseback. They all arrived and the boy showed them the hole he had dug. "From here I shot and hit him in the eye."

Along the road the people saw many animals, and little birds flying. The boy talked to the people, saying "These little birds don't do any harm to us. But those animals I made from the meat of the big bird, you must take care about those. From today on they are not going to be gentle. We no longer have danger from above. Now we must take care from below. These animals aren't much good for food, only for clothing. The birds are valuable only for their pretty feathers."

The men and the soldiers saw the bones of the big bird, and they went away contented, and in every pueblo began to make great fiestas.   MT

The Papago and Pima Indians tell of the slaying of a man-eating eagle which has some aspects in common with this myth (Densmore 1929: 45-54). The Cochiti also have a story about a cannibal eagle (Benedict 1931: 211).

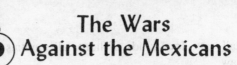

The Wars
Against the Mexicans

TOMAS CUPIZ traveled with his soldiers; there were forty. Beneath him was Francisco Flores, called Chico Matachini. His aide was Apolinar Pina, called Poli Soso'oki. These Indians left their families in the sierra of Chikurim in the care of Alejandro Rodrigues and Juan María Buitime'a and the old man, Paame'a. Tomas Cúpiz and his forty men went away, going down by way of Wicharubui in the direction of Torim. They crossed the river near Chu'umeampa'ako and from there went down to Wikicheba'am, the water hole of the birds. In this spot they killed animals for food, three burros, a mule, and two horses. They ate and carried the meat from these animals. They passed through the pueblo of Vicam which had been abandoned by its people. All of this occurred in the time after Madero, in 1912.

The men took water from the river and again took to the trail, slowly because of the great heat. It was the month of May. They neared Wicharubui and began to ascend the steep slope of the sierra. By the time they were half way across the sierra their canteens were empty of water. They tried to get water in the arroyo called Huchakowhoi. Every one seated himself on the rocks and rolled up his pant legs in preparation for the descent. There was great danger in the region of the water, for a detachment of federal soldiers, about four hundred men, was camped there. And the forty Yaquis had to have water from that arroyo. They left their packs of meat in the care of an old Yaqui called Belen, a relative of mine. Belen remained on guard on the top of the hill. Tomas Cúpiz and the others cautiously descended to the floor of the arroyo and began to drag themselves on their bellies in the direction of the water guarded by the federals. They were close to the soldiers when they stopped for a moment to catch their breath. The federals were not aware of them, although they were but three hundred meters away.

Tomas Cúpiz, lying flat on his belly, began to move a stone which he discovered loose before him. He pulled it up and beneath it was a small spring of beautiful, fresh water. All loosed the cups from their belts and drank to calm their thirst. Then they filled their canteens and also that of Belen. From there they retreated to the top of the rocky hill.

Belen, after drinking twice, spoke to them. "Since you went down, I have been hearing gun shots from the direction of Chikurim."

"What might they be doing to our families?" said Chico Matachini.

Immediately they shouldered their packs and set out in file. All were full of anger and they traveled swiftly. As they went down on the plain they met María Buitime'a who had been running, and behind him came Alejandro Rodrigues.

Then Poli Soso'oki asked of Alejandro, "What took place in Chikurim?"

Alejandro replied, "There arrived more than three hundred *pelones,* well armed, and they made pieces of us."

"And Paame'a?" asked Tomas Cúpiz.

"He was one of the first killed," replied Alejandro. "The only ones saved were ourselves and Rosalino Bakanawa and Rosalino Yolim'a and Tako Saruuki, for we ran."

"What of our families?" asked Pooli Pina.

"Let us go and give our families help. Shall it be this way or shall we make a turn by way of Ya'awimbwa'awa'apo?" said Chico Matachini.

Then answered Alejandro Rodrigues, "It is better that we turn that way."

"That we shall do," said the old man, Belen.

So they all retraced their steps down the same hill, passing near Wicharubui, in the direction of the disappearing sun. They took a small, flat stretch in the direction of the arroyo of Ayawimbwa'awakawi. They followed the arroyo from above. The sun had now set. They traveled laboriously through the craggy canyon. Without sleep they climbed toward the top of the hill. They kept marching without food or drink and in the early morning they arrived at Chikurim.

No one was to be seen. The federal soldiers had carried away some families and others were hidden in caves, in arroyos, and in the monte. Tomas Cúpiz and his men dispersed throughout the countryside searching out the wounded and dead and the frightened women. Children were dying of thirst. The first encountered by Tomas Cúpiz was a young girl called Sewakame. She lay beneath a small tree that cast no shade and was almost dead. He took her in his arms and placed her in the shade and gave her water.

Alejandro and Juan María Buitime'a built a fire to cook meat and feed the people. Others walked in search of the dead, to burn them. José Kome'ela, a cousin of mine, and others brought in a number of girls they had found, also nearly dead of hunger and thirst. When the meat was cooked, they made a broth with which to nourish them. And soon the families were removed to the southern part of the sierra Bacatete.

War Between the Yaquis and the Pimas

LIKE ALL OTHER tribes, the Pimas recognized the Yaquis as their supreme authority. However, in life no thing is perfect nor lasting; so it happened that one day at the fiesta celebrating San Juan's day, the Yaquis and the Pimas had a terrible quarrel. The fiesta was taking place near the hill of Echoakame. The trouble was caused by a trifle, a mean little act.

The Pimas wanted permission to borrow the image of San Juan from the Yaquis in order that they might carry it to their pueblo, that is, to Onabachi. But the Yaquis flatly denied them the privilege. There was a great discussion and the disgruntled Pimas then retired to their homeland, some to No'obachi, others to Onabachi, Tonichi, or Nu'uram.

A few days later the Pimas sent an emissary to see the Yaqui leaders, carrying the ultimatum that if the Yaquis would not allow them the use of their saint, the Pima tribe would rise in arms and take San Juan by force.

The Yaquis answered only that they were ready to receive the Pimas.

Three weeks later, over six hundred Pimas came toward the Yaqui territory in warlike guise, well armed with bows and arrows and lances.

A scout who was guarding the Yaqui territory, saw the Pimas approaching. He immediately informed his chief, who then armed many Yaquis in readiness for the encounter.

The Pimas attacked suddenly and with great force. The Yaqui soldiers were well armed and equipped, and excellent marksmen. They fought for some time. Finally the Pimas, seeing such resistance in their enemy, began to retreat and abandon the field. The Yaquis, in mass, followed them, and pushed them at the point of their arrows to a place called El Realito.

There the Yaquis mounted a long, low hill. They camped at one end of the mesa. The Pimas camped at the other end of the mesa, among a small clump of trees. Night fell, with neither the Pimas or the Yaquis showing any battle. As it darkened, the Yaquis could see a multitude of little lights such as those of cigarette coals at the Pima camp. It appeared as if all of the Pimas were smoking. The Yaquis realized that there were many Pimas, and they said to one another, "Let us go after them in the early morning."

At four in the morning, the Yaquis started toward the Pima encampment. Before six they arrived at the spot where they had seen the cigarettes burning the night before. But they encountered no one—not even the ashes of the cigarettes which had been smoked.

"What does this mean?" asked Cocheme'a.

"It means that those Pimas are wizards and that they have tricked us. They left yesterday, after resting, and only their witcheries remained here to keep us occupied," said Naawa.

Peace at Pitahaya

Pitahaya, Rio Yaqui, January 9, 1909

PEACE WAS made at Pitahaya with the eight pueblos of this tribe while Luis Buli was General of the Yaquis. Yzábal was governor, and the generals of the Mexican forces were Lorenzo Torres and Luis Torres. Also there were some people from North America as representatives at this peace. A party of Papagos attended. They came as witches in order to do harm to the Yaquis. That is why Yzábal won this peace.

Yzábal brought with him a Padre to bless the laying down of the Yaquis' arms. On the eighth day they began to discuss the peace. Yzábal and Luis Torres and Lorenzo Torres questioned the pueblos concerning how to make this peace. The old men of our tribe said that they should set up a cross for the swearing of the oaths. They said that two persons from each side should be named to swear the peace and an image should be placed between those two persons during the taking of the oaths. That was the form in which the peace should be arranged. And so it was done.

The people of the government numbered sixty thousand. The whole valley of Pitahaya was covered with soldiers as far back as the sierra. Of the Yaquis, there numbered 90 men.

The Mexican soldiers placed out two boxes, one for our equipment and one for our arms. And they began to disarm the Yaquis. Yzábal said to Luis Buli, "Now you will be disarmed, all of your people. These arms must be blessed, for they have sinned. They have killed many people," said the generals of the government. "Now you are in our power. God has punished you," they said to Luis Buli.

Then Luis Buli said to them, "You did not inform me of this yesterday during our arrangement of the peace. Therefore, I cannot order that these arms be turned over to you." These were the words of General Luis Buli.

The Mexican generals began to order movement of their troops. We were surrounded by double columns. They began to disarm the Yaquis. They came to two men of General Buli's guard to disarm them. These two men attacked Yzábal, their bayonets drawn, and said to him, "Keep your word as the peace was made!"

Yzábal and Luis Torres gaped with their mouths wide open. The other Torres shouted for order. And we of the federation who had all gathered round were quieted. This took place near the village of Pitahaya.

Of those two men of this unhappy tribe, one fell in the following battle. His name is acclaimed in our memories. He was Santiago Guicoyoi. The second was Tiburcio Agraciamacqui. These are the two men who put their bayonets at the breast of the generals of the government.

Yzábal died of fright in some state in Europe after soiling his pants during the peace pact at Pitahaya. This is very positive in our history.   JV

Malinero'okai

THE SPANIARDS had just entered the Yaqui sierra. It was just when they battled the Indians in the heights of the Batachim sierra that Malinero' okai, with her little girl, descended into the depths of a canyon at the foot of the hill where they were fighting.

Malinero'okai was frightened because never in her life had she heard the sound of fire-arms which now echoed in the heart of the hills. Quickly she took up her baby girl whom she carried in a cradle of skins made from the wolves her husband had hunted. The valiant Ta'a Himsi, her husband, also was in battle. Malinero'okai was afraid and alone with her little girl, the beautiful Aaki Sewa. She wrapped the little one in wildcat skin and put her on her shoulders. She took a long stick and she walked down the rocky, water-less arroyo. As she traveled thus she contemplated the cliffs and occasional fronds of *kauchunam*. These enchanting trees reminded her that she and her husband had passed by here two weeks before.

95

The Stories

She traveled thus, out of the Batachim sierra in the morning of that day. It was the hot month of August, and she traveled without stopping even a moment to take a drop of the fresh cool shade of the leafy trees. In the afternoon, Malinero'okai arrived where there was a bit of water, at a place where the arroyo made a sharp turn.

Taking the child from her shoulders, she placed her in the shade of a tree. She, herself, took some water and then cut some grass and branches for a bed. She lay down beside her little girl and, together, they passed the rest of the afternoon. Later she again set out and walked until night had come. In the midst of darkness she found refuge under some branches and spent the night there. She was accompanied by the songs of birds of night, the howl of coyotes and the cry of the tiger as she quietly fed her child. Those animals did not cause her to fear for she was used to hearing them all her life.

The following morning very early she hunted some fruits and roots and ate them with good appetite. The little girl, Aaki Sewa, who was scarcely three months old, rested as her mother ate. The mother said to her, "Would you like to eat some fruit?" And she offered it to her, but at the same time she added, "No, you may not eat them because you are very little and it might do you some harm and your father would be angry."

That morning, with the freshness, Malinero' okai took to the road at a good pace. She was young and strong, agile at climbing and descending the heights and depths of the trail. At midday she found herself at the waterhole which is both enchanting and enchanted. It lies at the foot of

some cliffs called the pillars. The Spanish call it
pilares. But the Yaquis call this water-hole *pilaesi'im*. It is a great eye of water, profoundly deep
and it never goes dry. The Yaquis say that it
is really an enchanted pueblo which was con-
verted into water. Here, Malinero'okai came, and
she encountered some families she knew. They
were all very glad to see her. They offered her
atole of pechitas and of mesquites. As she rested,
she talked with an intimate friend of hers, "You
who are an old woman and know something, tell
me, Wiru Masa, is it certain that this waterhole
is an enchanted pueblo?"

"Yes, it is the pueblo of the oldest Indians.
I don't know if they were Yaquis or Surem. But
your disbelief will be dispersed."

Effectively, at seven in the evening they heard
noises. They heard the calls of little boys and
the sound of a violin. The two women went down
to the shore of the pool but they saw nothing there
except a gourd and some watermelons. They
heard the sound of the *teneboim* worn by pascolas
as they danced. And many laughs. Then all at
once all stopped.

"Now you know," said Wiru Masa.

"Yes," said Malinero'okai.

The two women retired to their camping
place. They were chatting like friends when they
heard the word. It was quite late at night. The
word was spoken softly, *"Dios'em chani'abu."*

"Dios'em chi'okwe," answered the women.
The recently arrived ones were two Yaqui men
who had been fighting in the Batachim sierra.
Having been greeted, they were allowed to come
up to the women's camp.

Malinero'okai asked about her husband, Ta'a Himsi. And the others asked about their husbands.

"Ta'a Himsi was killed," said one of the men whose name was Wikoa Wikia. "Ta'a Himsi died out there in the afternoon. That is all we know."

"The Spaniards we chased to Otam Kaki. They turned back on us and killed some Yaquis. But on that hill and on the other hill also we killed many of them."

"This I knew, my Dios told me," said Malinero'okia. "My man, so young and valiant." With profound sadness the young girl spoke.

On the following morning Wikoa Wikia said to the women, "It would be better if all of you left here for Wicho'em or returned to Tabero Ba'am. Or, we could take you to Nabo Hakia or to Sibam. It is very pretty country there, more beautiful than here. There is much grass and wild food. Here are many dangers. Those who live in these water-holes are evil. Only wizards and devil-makers live here and if they should awake in bad humor they would harm you. They may turn into animals, or they may strike at you from the depths of the water. Also there is another very sure danger here," added Wikoa Wikia. "When it rains this arroyo fills with water. If you stay here you risk all these dangers. So tell me to which place you would like to go."

"Take us to Sibam."

Thus they set out, leaving Pilaesi'm. In order to reach Sibam they traveled three days. It is quite distant, Sibam, away to the north.

In three days they arrived at another water-hole, new homes, new surroundings, happy and enjoyable, for now they had time to make homes and they had many new neighbors.

All was beautiful except for Malinero'okai. For her all was sad. Every day she became sadder. She didn't want to eat. She cried for Ta'a Himsi. The valiant Ta'a Himsi. Finally she died.

Her little girl, Aaki Sewa, was taken over by her friends who brought her up until she was a grown and beautiful girl.

Colorin colorado

Castro says, "This bit of history was told me by an old lady named Mayo Juriana who is a direct descendant of Malinero'okai."

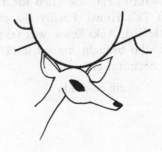

The First Deer Hunter

THIS is the story of the first Yaqui deer hunter. He is called Yebu'uku Yoeme. This man, since he was very young, lived alone with his mother in a place called Poobetame'aka'apo.

Yebu'uku Yoeme was a very good hunter. He had great power over the deer. He dominated them so that they became as tame as burros. The deer were very wild and dangerous, but Yebu'uku Yoeme could catch up with them and tame them. Sometimes he would tie two together and drive them like a team.

Throughout his youth, he didn't know another person except his mother, only animals and the monte. He didn't do anything except to bring his mother water from the lagoon near their house, and then go out into the monte among the animals.

After many years, a beautiful young girl appeared to Yebu'uku Yoeme. The story does not say where she came from or whose daughter she was—only that she came from the seashore to the north. Her name was Seahamut.

Before dawn, she arrived at the water hole where Yebu'uku Yoeme was accustomed to draw water for his mother. Seahamut had begun to wash her hair when Yebu'uku arrived. He said to her, "Good morning, woman."

"Good morning, man," answered Seahamut.

"Why do you wash in the water that I drink?" he asked.

"I don't know," answered the girl.

"Where do you come from?" asked Yebu'uku Yoeme.

And she replied, "I don't know that either. I am lost. I don't know who I am, or where I came from. I am only walking about lost. But I came here," said Seahamut, with a happy smile on her lips. "Where do you live, man?"

"Not far," answered Yebu'uku Yoeme.

"Have you no mother?" she asked.

"Yes, I have."

"Then why do you have to carry water?"

"I don't know," said Yebu'uku Yoeme.

"Take me to your house and I will live with you," said the girl.

"Come with me," said Yebu'uku Yoeme, and he took her to the patio of his house. "Wait here a moment. I am going to ask permission of my mother," he said, and he put her behind some green branches.

Seahamut said, "Tell your mother that you want very much to get married. Then she will ask you where you are going to find a woman. Tell her that you just found one, and then both of you come here for me."

The mother of Yebu'uku Yoeme was sweeping her house. It was early in the morning.

Yebu'uku Yoeme said to his mother, "Mother I have a great desire to get married."

"My dear son, where will I find a girl for you here? There are none, and I don't know where I can find you one!"

"I know where there is one," said Yebu'uku Yoeme.

"Take me to her," said the mother.

They both went to the place where Seahamut was hiding. When the girl saw them coming, she came out to meet them.

The mother said to her, "Come to our house. From now on it is yours. From today on, you must clean it daily." She led her to the kitchen. "Here is the olla. You will bring fresh water every day. From now on the house is in your charge. This is your husband. He was carrying water because he had no woman, but today that task falls to you. He will go into the monte and hunt the deer and bring you food. That will now be his only work to hunt the deer."

Well they were very happily married until they both died of old age.

Tepecano mythology records an incident of a boy finding a girl at a lake, bringing her to the patio and requesting his mother to come out and greet his wife.

The Death of Kutam Tawi

THERE LIVED in the pueblo of Potam a Yaqui captain named Tawachime'a. He had been a captain a long time when he married a very beautiful native girl with an enchanting appearance who was called Kuku Tosa, which means Dove Nest. From this marriage a very handsome little Yaqui boy resulted.

As soon as this little boy was born, the captain Tawachime'a called together all of those men who were wise, those who knew how to divine certain things. He had them come to his hut, and he asked them to tell him what the destiny of his son would be, what luck was he to expect during his life. Above all, what was going to cause the boy's death and how long was he going to live. All of this, Tawachime'a desired to know.

Well, these intelligent men were united there for three days in order to divine. On the third day an ancient Yaqui named Chikul, which means Rat, presented himself to the captain. "Do you truly wish to know?"

"Yes, Chikul," said the captain.

Then the old man, Chikul, seated himself on a log of cottonwood and he said, "Your son will be very intelligent but his destiny is bad. When he is fifteen years old, at midday, your son will die at the hands of a stranger."

Tawachime'a was studying in his mind how, in what manner, his only son might escape death. The son was called Kutam Tawi.

"However, continued Chikul, "this boy, if he is not dead at the age of fifteen, will live to the age of sixty-three."

The captain Tawachime'a gave credit to the

ancient, for he knew that Chikul never told a lie. He brought out two bags. From one he took some native tobacco, *hiakbeibam*. He gave this to Chikul. From the other sack he took many discs of pure silver. And he said, "Chikul, take this little gift." And he gave Chikul the silver. Chikul took the gift and gave his thanks. Then the woman of Tawachime'a, Kuku Tosa, brought out an olla full of bee's honey and another full of wild seeds and a pair of tiger skins. She said to Chikul, "May Dios bless you."

"Many thanks," said the wise Chikul, and retired to his hut.

The young man, Kutam Tawi, grew. Eight days before he would be fifteen years of age, Tawachime'a and Kuku Tosa took him to the hill named Tohkobi 'iku. There they arrived, close to the foot of the sierra. Scratching the ground with his foot from side to side, Tawachime'a found a large flat stone. He took up the stone and they went down into a tunnel. An hour or so later Tawachime'a and Kuku Tosa came out again. They left Kutam Tawi there in order to save him from death.

But near-by a young Yaqui was hidden. He had just hidden there, filled with fear because of a struggle with some bad Yaquis. He had run away in order to escape sure death. The bad Yaquis were looking for him, saying, "Wherever you go, we'll get you out!" Thus the young Yaqui had come to hide close to the tunnel.

When Tawachime'a and Kuku Tosa had gone far away, the young man came out of his hiding place, opened the cave, entered and covered the entrance with the same stone. He presented himself to Kutam timidly, saying, "Please excuse me, brother, but I come here frightened. Some Yaquis want to kill me. Let me hide with you until I get over my fright and my enemies leave."

"Stay here with me," said Kutam Tawi. "My parents brought me here to stay until I am fifteen years old. It is foretold a stranger may kill me."

"And how many days until you are fifteen?"

"Six days," answered Kutam Tawi.

"Well, I must not stay here. I don't want to kill anyone."

"If you kill me, it would be the will of Dios. Stay here and be my companion until the day fixed for my death."

When the fatal day arrived, the boy Kutam Tawi was reposing on some lion skins. It was twelve minutes before twelve. He would die at twelve; thus was the prediction. Kutam Tawi, lying there, said to Kama Wiroa, "Will you bring me my spear."

The weapon was a piece of wood with a very fine point. Kama Wiroa picked up the spear. On coming up to Kutam Tawi, he tripped and fell. The weapon struck into the boy's heart, killing him instantly.

Kama Wiroa knelt on his knees and wept bitterly. He was weeping when Tawachime'a and Kuku Tosa arrived. They entered to find the young Yaqui kneeling and crying out loudly, "I have become a criminal without wishing it."

"Be it as Dios desires," they said.

They picked up the dead boy, and Kama Wiroa accompanied them to Potam where they buried him after a great fiesta and ceremony. Here ends this story.

The Flood and the Prophets

HERE PRESENTED is what was adopted for the martyrology of the period of the universal flood. Out of this catastrophe were saved those from whom sprang the generations of Yaitowi, a just and perfect man.

Yaitowi, in his time, walked with Dios when came to pass the days when waters rose over the earth to destroy all living things, alike beneath the sky, on the earth, and living in the water— even the birds who fly over the earth in the open expanse of the sky. It so happened that on the seventh day of February the flood waters covered the earth. In this time of Yaitowi, in the year 614, the day of the 17th of that same month of February, it rained all over the world. This continued for fourteen days and fourteen nights. Since the blessed end, every thing that had been alive, and all life substance was thus finished. The waters increased hugely over all the earth, destroying all living things, after the days of men and women were terminated.

And on the seventeenth of the month of July the waters were receding until the first of October, when the tops of the hills showed. And the first day of November, the water retired from the world's surface. Yaitowi and thirteen others as well as eleven women were saved on the hill of Parbus, which today is called Maatale. And on the hill of Jonas, eleven souls and one woman called Emac Dolores were saved. The woman disappeared in the seventh year, turning into a statue of stone, now Mount Matuakame.

On Egosin hill, now called Tosalkawi, six were saved, and three from Mount Tohowai, called today Rehepakawi.

On Golgota, now named Te'etpa'aria, Fou Emac and two more were saved. From Otameahui and the Sinaii sierra, now called Samawaaka, a man named Vaculo and a woman, Domicilia who is an angel, seven birds, and seven asses, and seven little dogs were saved. Also from the sierra of Vaber, now Totoitakuse'epo, a man called Ekitoyis and a woman, Paresenobix survived.

After these events, it came to pass that two angels arrived at the hills of Sinai at the break of dawn. Vaculo and Fou Emac were seated on a stone, singing the Holy Hymn. On seeing the angels, they arose to receive them, bowing toward the ground and toward the sky. They addressed the angels, "Well, gentlemen, sent by your God to this valley of tears, we beg that you defend us."

The angels said, "All difficult things may be done by Dios. At the assigned time one comes after who has made the road of Dios straight. And we will return here according to the time of your lives."

And on the seventh day, when morning came, there was thunder and lightning and thick clouds all over the hills. It was seen that in those days the angel San Gabriel came, sent by Dios, saying to Vaculo and Fou Emac and Serafina, "Repent, for the reign of the king of the heavens, of the holies, of the altar is close. For this is the one of whom was spoken by the prophet. *Indomin patricin* and go by the way of our Dios and Father." They went.

And they arrived at the place called Venedici. And they heard the voice of Dios, "And I, Dios, bless Vaculo, Fou Emac and Serafina, and I will spread the blood of man because man is made in the image of Dios. Now there will be no more flood to destroy the earth, which is a sign. For centuries I will put my arch in the clouds. When I cause clouds to come over the earth, I will allow my arch to be seen. Remember me, and today my arch will be on the altar and in the second tabernacle of Dios, to remind me of my pact between myself and all living souls."

And they said to Dios, "What do you want us to do?" And they said, "Give us some of your glory in our holy altar."

And Dios spoke to them. "You may drink from the glass from which I drink." And he commenced to speak, "Take care that no one deceives you. This is my house of prayer. You will be called by all kinds of men who are false prophets. There are many caves of thieves. If one speaks to you, saying, 'I am Dios,' do not believe him. They carry false testimony. Brothers against brothers, parents against children will kill one another. And the false prophets will read you signs to deceive you. And at a time foretold, Rahbonix will come."

These are our ancient, chronological generations, the years which completed the end, the known deeds to which we refer in this general table of ancient law and letters as told by Ynexselci deo mamfin.

The correctness of the Holy Trinity, garden of Dios (which is now Potam), is known. In Eden, now Bacum, our Mother, Saint Rosalie, was the marvelous apparition of the year 707.

And likewise in the year 902 was seen the marvelous vision of the Holy Cross in Venedicit, which today is Abascaure. Finally comes the incarnate birth of our Father, Jesucristo, redeemer of the world.

After these things, in the year 1414 to 1417, Andreas Kowame, Isiderio Sinsai, Andres Quizo, and Rabdi Kowame appeared. Rabdi Kowame preached to those who accompanied him that day, the sixth of the first month of the innocent children of 1414. "Travel over all of the forests, hills, and villages to come out at a place called Takalaim. Preach the holy division line and announce the gospel of the reign of God." And he said, "Go ahead, do honor, and preach the Holy Hymn."

Passing on from there a little farther, they arrived at Cocoraqui, where they taught the holy doctrine and commandments of Dios. Leaving Cocoraqui, en route to Cabora, Rabdi Kowame says, *"Eli Eli lama sabactani,"* which means, "My Lord, come forth and do honor."

Proceeding from there, and farther on, arriving at Cabora, he speaks again to those who accompany him, "Watch that no one deceives you, for many men will come, and he will deceive you, 'I am he, sent by Dios,' and he will deceive many of you and our children. Do not hear those who come after this. War will be seen, and we will be upset, and there will be no end." JV

San Pedro and Cristo

ONE TIME San Pedro and Jesucristo were walking along, and Jesucristo sent San Pedro up to a near-by house to get a cooked chicken. On the way back Pedro ate one leg of the chicken.

When Jesucristo saw what San Pedro had brought back, he asked, "Why has this chicken but one leg?"

"It never had another leg," answered Pedro. "All of the chickens around this part of the country have but one leg, Sir."

The two proceeded and came to a big tree under which were sleeping many chickens. All of the chickens had one leg tucked up out of sight under their feathers.

Pedro pointed to them and said, "You see! All of the chickens have but one leg apiece."

Jesucristo took a rock and threw it at one of the chickens. It woke up and stood on both feet.

"Oh," said Pedro, "A miracle!" He then took up a rock and threw it at the rest of the chickens. "You see," he said, "I can perform miracles, too."

Jesucristo and San Pedro

JESUCRISTO walked about talking with sick men. When Lazaro was dead, Jesucristo brought him to life.

San Pedro was always envious thinking how sad it was that Jesucristo never charged a fee for his services in curing and bringing people to life. "Oh, how sad," he thought. "If it had been I who cured Lazaro I should have asked a great deal of money." He was wondering if perhaps he couldn't bring the dead to life as Jesucristo did.

They walked to another pueblo, arriving at an early hour. Jesucristo cured some people there and San Pedro was still hoping that he would charge a little fee.

Jesucristo taught the people about curing. "This herb has the power to cure snake bite," he said. In this way he taught the Yaquis.

San Pedro wanted also to cure as did Jesucristo. By now he had learned all of the prayers and how to gesture as Jesucristo did. One day he hid from the others. He walked to a place where a sick man lived, for he wanted to make a cure all by himself. San Pedro performed something like an operation on this man, making many motions and prayers, and using some cure. The hour came and passed, and San Pedro could not revive the patient. He was frightened. He left, calling on Dios for help with all his heart. He found Jesucristo and said to him, "I need you. I could not revive my patient."

"Very well," said Jesucriso, and he went to the place where the dead man was. He put out his hand and said, "Rise up, José," and the dead man came to life.

San Pedro is always very quick to beg pardon. He asked forgiveness of Jesucristo and of course he was pardoned.

San Pedro did not continue in this capricious way. Now he is very good at curing; but always with the help of Jesucristo.   LC

Pedro de Ordimales

PEDRO DE ORDIMALES and Jesucristo were walking along a road. Pedro, who was following behind, picked some figs and put them in his bag, not mentioning the action to Cristo. When he was hungry, he reached into the bag and pulled out a fig and ate it. Jesucristo, without turning around, said, "What are you eating, Pedro?"

"Oh, just some burro excrement, sir."

A little later Pedro de Ordimales was hungry again and reached into his bag for another fig. He pulled out a piece of burro dung.

Cycles of stories about Pedro de Ordimales (or Urdimales) have spread from Europe to the Spanish American population of this continent and are common today. For a discussion of their distribution see: Espinosa 1914b: 220-221; Mason and Espinosa 1914: 166-171, 206-207.

113

The Stories

San Pedro
and
the Devil

JESUCRISTO had many apostles and prophets the Devil was constantly trying to tempt. Jesucristo would help them and give them advice.

One day San Pedro was standing by a big cottonwood tree. The Devil came up to him and said, "I hear that you are very powerful. I, also, am very strong. If you can strike this tree with your fist so that your hand goes through the trunk from one side to the other, I will admit that you are stronger than me."

"Very well," said San Pedro, "but not right now, señor. Tomorrow."

Jesucristo came to the spot and San Pedro consulted with him. Jesucristo bored a hole through the tree trunk and then covered up all evidence of it.

The next day Jesucristo appeared at the contest and volunteered to act as judge. He tapped the trunk and showed the contestants where to strike.

First, he tapped a solid place and said to the Devil, "You try first."

The Devil struck the tree trunk and his hand

entered only a few inches. Then San Pedro struck the trunk on the spot indicated by Jesucristo. His arm went all the way through.

But the Devil was stubborn and always came back to try again. One day he said to San Pedro, "I'll bring two spears and we will contest to see which of us can throw one the farthest toward the other side of the sea."

"Good, we will meet tomorrow," said San Pedro. Then he consulted with Jesucristo.

On the hour, the Devil appeared before San Pedro with two spears. The two stood on the seashore ready to throw. But when the Devil raised his spear, it spoke, saying, "Spear, go to France and enter the body of the mother of the Devil!"

"No, no!" said the Devil, lowering his arm and letting the spear fall to the ground. So again the Devil lost.

Another day the Devil said to San Pedro, "Come here. The one who throws a rock the farthest toward that island on the other side of the sea wins."

San Pedro agreed. Jesucristo helped him. When they were both standing ready, the Devil reached down and picked up a stone. San Pedro reached into his pocket and pulled out something.

"Are you ready?" asked the Devil.

"Yes," replied San Pedro. Together, they threw. The Devil's rock fell into the sea but San Pedro's disappeared far into the distance. It was a little gray quail.

"Again you win over me!" he said.   LC

Stories featuring San Pedro as a crafty character are widespread in Mexico.

The Stories

Father Frog

WHEN A YAQUI man who is old and well off lies on his death bed, it is the custom for his family to gather about him. Sometimes one of his sons will ask the sick man, "If you should die in whose hands would you leave your land?"

"Who is my best friend?" asks the man.

With the hope of being left the inheritance all answer, *"Nehpo, Nehpo, Nehpo,"* which means, "I, I, I."

Then the old man asks, "Who among you will accompany me then when I die?"

No one answers.

It is thus among all of the animals too, even down to the little frogs. The father frog, on his death bed, asks, "Who is my best friend?"

And all of the little frogs answer, *"Nehpo, Nehpo, Nehpo."*

You have heard them. LC

Two Little Lambs

LONG AGO there were two little lambs who were not quite full grown. They were walking about out in the country in the sierra on a large plain, when a very hungry coyote walked out of the forest and came straight toward one of them. "How are you, cousin?" said the coyote.

"Very well, my cousin," answered the lamb.

"I come to you very hungry, little one."

The lamb said, "What might I give you to eat? I am eating grass. But you don't understand eating grass as I do."

"No, I do not like grass. But I would like to eat you, little cousin."

"Don't eat me," said the lamb, looking afar off. "Over there is one who is much fatter. Let us go over to him."

"Yes, he is very fat. We will go over there."

The coyote and the lamb started off together toward the other lamb, and the first lamb said to the coyote, "Wait for me a minute." And he took the other lamb apart while the coyote stood there and waited.

The first lamb said to the second, "Coyote wants to eat us. But we are going to trick him. Let us each go away a distance and have a race. You go toward where the sun is going down. I will go toward where the sun rises, over there I will go. Then coyote will call us and we will run toward him and when we come together, we will gore him quickly and tear him apart with our horns. This way we will kill him."

"Good," said the other lamb.

Then they went up to the coyote and thus they spoke to him, "Here we are, together. Together we will run a race, and he who wins, that lamb you may eat."

One lamb marked a line on the ground with his hoof. "Stand here, little cousin coyote. I am going over there toward where the sun goes down. My brother is going toward where the sun comes up, and we will both stop. When you call to us we will race here, toward you. He who wins, you will eat."

"Very fine," said the coyote. He was happily jumping about and singing and dancing and think-ing of eating the little lamb.

The two lambs each went far off and stopped. Then the coyote, who was watching them, called out. The two started running toward him. Equal distance they neared him, and together, they arrived upon him, caught him in the center and gored him. Together, they tore him and gored him. Coyote was finished.

There you have it, my fathers.

Maisoka and Hima'awikia

MAISOKA was in his house one day and about the time that he stuck his head out of his door, Hima'awikia was walking about. Maisoka said, "Who walks on top of the house of the King?" He said this because he considered himself a king.

Maisoka means tarantula. It is an animal which is black and has a number of legs and a bit of hair. He lives in the ground, making a house in the ground, as do the snakes. He puts a top on his hole, which is the door to his house.

Hima'awikia is an insect with wings. It is a little animal, a bit reddish and it flies. This is he who walked over the home of Maisoka making a noise with his wings, going thus: "rururu."

Maisoka heard the "ronronrcn" and he stuck his head out and said, "Who is this imposter who walks on the roof of the house of the King?"

"Oh, pardon me, Sir," said Hima'awikia, and Maisoka allowed him to enter his house.

A few minutes later Hima'awikia came out carrying Maisoka between his teeth. It appears unbelievable that Hima'awikia, who is so small, always conquers Maisoka and eats him. Maisoka never escapes from the teeth of Hima'awikia.

*The
Stories*

The Cricket and the Lion

EARLY one morning a young lion was out taking a walk through the fresh monte when suddenly he came upon a large plain and a big lagoon full of fresh, crystal water. After looking for a while, he went on his way. He stopped and grubbed in a little hill of dry trash, and out of it jumped a cricket. The lion wanted to crush him with his heavy hand, but the lively cricket jumped from one side to the other and sang thus: "chik chik chik."

The lion said to him, "Who are you?"

"I am the chief of a tribe more valiant than you or your tribe, answered the cricket. And he kept on singing "chik chik chik."

The lion replied, "You want to make fun of me, but you are mistaken. I am the king of the forest, of all of the big and the brave animals. They are good soldiers, and strong."

"My soldiers are not very big in stature, but in valor, they are immense, braver than all the tigers, wolves, and lions!" said the cricket.

"I am displeased," said the lion. "Today I declare war on you."

"My troops are ready," said the cricket, "chik chik chik chik."

"Here, close to this lagoon, we will meet tomorrow," said the lion, shaking his head.

It was winter-time. The lion went into the forest and gathered together the animals of the claw, lions, tigers, wolves, coyotes, and many other felines.

The cricket went to some bee-hives. To the bees he said, "Go and advise all of your companions of the wing that we will fight the people of the claw." So the bees called up all the insects that fly and sting, and also the scorpions and ants. All met on the plain where the battle was to take place so that all the ground was covered with them. The insects hid among the stalks and among the branches. There, they awaited the day.

Early in the morning, the cricket and the lion met. The cricket was accompanied by four cockroaches and six Granddaddy-long-leg spiders. The lion was accompanied by four coyotes, seven wolves, and many other animals of the claw.

"Where are your soldiers?" asked the lion of the cricket.

"Don't ask me any questions. Let us battle!" said the cricket.

"Come on, boys!" shouted the lion. And all of the animals entered upon the plain.

The ants and scorpions broke up out of the earth and commenced to bite the paws of the soldiers of the lion. Wherever one might look came the tiny animals with their tails pointed. The bees and hornets came in like a cloud, and they began to bite the mouths, tails, and eyes of the enemy. The cats found no way to defend themselves and howled with pain and leapt high in the air. And the insects attacked more violently, covering the entire bodies of the animals, climbing over them and biting them many times. The big animals cried from pain and fear. Desperately they ran and threw themselves into the water.

The insects retired to the branches, and the lion ordered the coyote to go out and scout to see if those little birds of the devil were still somewhere about.

The coyote walked out a little way and shouted, "Do you give in?" Then to the lion he said, "They are finished." He had no sooner said this than a troop of hornets descended on him. He ran and fell again into the lagoon.

The animals stayed in the water all day until night arrived. At last they came out, the lions, tigers, bears, and wolves, all the people of the claw. They stepped very softly and quickly, going to the forest with no desires ever again to battle with the insects.

Yaquis say that there is no small enemy. Everyone can defend himself. The cricket continues to sing, "chik chik chik." He is not afraid.

Grasshopper and Cricket

THE CRICKET invited the grasshopper, saying, "Let's go over to that banquet. We will see lots of wine. I'll get you some wine to drink and then we can ride horseback all night long through the monte singing."

"Well, let's go," said the grasshopper, and they went to the banquet.

The cricket said to the grasshopper, "Sit down here on this little stick. I am going to get you some wine." The cricket went over to where they were serving wine and jumped into a cup of it. The Chief saw the cricket in the cup and threw the wine over toward the grasshopper. He bathed the grasshopper in wine.

"Good, isn't it?" asked the cricket.

"Delicious," answered the grasshopper.

Together they went away. They encountered a lion who was lying down. They climbed up on top of him, singing. The lion, who was angry at being disturbed, got up and walked away, trying to get away from the sound of the singing. But the cricket and the grasshopper climbed out on the end of the lion's tail and sang all night long as the lion walked about.

Finally the lion got tired of the singing and switched his tail and threw off the grasshopper and the cricket and he went away into the monte to lie down for a rest.

The old Yaquis say that now the lion keeps his distance from the grasshopper and the cricket. He hides in places where there is no *chik chik chik* to disturb his sleep.

123

Turtle and Coyote

ONE DAY IN the very hot month of August, the season of picking pitahayas, a turtle was walking along under the branches of the pitahaya plants. She was eating from the pitahayas which were ripe and which had fallen to the ground. She was walking along with her mouth all red from pitahaya juice.

As she walked along, she came upon a hungry coyote. The coyote greeted her very courteously, and asked, "What is it that you have eaten which makes your mouth all red?"

"I just ate a man. And if you bother me, I shall eat you too," the turtle replied, opening her mouth and showing her teeth.

The coyote was frightened. After some time he said, "Friend turtle, tell me where I can find something to eat."

"Come with me. At a big ranch I have some friends. They always feed me. And everything they give me will be for you." Chatting thus, they walked along. The coyote and the turtle had been walking for some time when the coyote, desperate with hunger, said, "When are we going to arrive at this ranch? Is it very much farther?"

"No, no, it isn't far," answered the turtle. But this was a lie, for there was no ranch at all.

They went on walking for a long time. Again the coyote asked, "Is it far away?"

"No, not far," answered Madame Turtle, walking at her own pace, very slowly. And the coyote, about to fall down from hunger, said to the turtle, "Why don't you walk just a bit faster?"

"Oh," said the turtle, "I can't walk very fast. When I travel fast, smoke begins to rise from my feet. Look at my feet and you'll see there is no smoke under them at all."

The coyote put his nose down and walked behind the turtle, looking at her feet—and dying of hunger. Finally the coyote fell down in a faint, without strength. He did not eat the turtle, nor did he eat at the ranch, nor did he ever see smoke rise from the turtle's feet. He died. And the turtle went on walking.

This took place in the very beginning of the world, when the coyote was more silly than he is now, the most ignorant of all the animals.

Coyote and Rabbit

ONE DAY rabbit was out on a plain eating when Coyote came up. "I am very hungry," said Coyote. "I am going to eat you."

"No, wait here and I will bring you a really good meal of chicken. They are cooking it over there." Rabbit ran off toward the monte and Coyote happily waited, singing in anticipation of a fine meal. He waited a long time. At last he became angry and followed the tracks of Rabbit.

He found Rabbit in an arroyo standing by the cliff wall holding his forepaws against the cliff. "What are you doing?" asked Coyote.

"I am holding this cliff up," said Rabbit. At that moment a little rock fell and he held the cliff up harder than ever. "Here," he said to Coyote, "you hold it up while I go and get the food I told you about. It is almost ready."

Coyote put his paws against the cliff, pushing desperately while Rabbit ran off. Another rock fell and Coyote pushed all the harder. He waited for a long time. He was very tired and terribly hungry. Suddenly he let go of the cliff and ran as fast as he could. Nothing happened. He followed the tracks of Rabbit.

'Now I really am going to eat you!"

"Just sit down," said Rabbit. "They are going to bring that food right here. They'll be here soon." So Coyote sat down, looking hungrily at Rabbit. Rabbit jumped up saying, "I'll hurry them. You wait here just a minute." He ran off. Coyote waited.

Meanwhile, Rabbit set fire all around the edges of the thicket. Then he ran back to Coyote. "Hear the *cohetes?*" he shouted to Coyote. "The fiesta is coming. They are bringing you a wonderful meal." Then Rabbit ran away as fast as he could to avoid the fire. Coyote happily danced and sang as he waited for his meal. The fire soon surrounded him and he was burned up.

The above incident and others form a cycle of tales which has a wide distribution among the Latin Americans of Mexico and Southwestern United States (Espinosa 1914b: 211-212). Also, incidents featuring various animals are found among widely separated American Indian groups as, for instance, the Tepecanos of Mexico (Mason and Espinosa 1914: 204), the Cochiti of New Mexico (Benedict 1935: 308), and the Papagos of Arizona (Jane Chesky, Field Notes 1942).

Heron and Fox

IN THE DAYS when animals talked proper Yaqui, a fox and a heron formed an intimate friendship.

The fox, in order to show her sharpness and wit, said to the heron one day, "Do come and visit me tomorrow."

"I will," answered the heron.

The following day the heron flew to the foot of a little hill where the fox had her cave. "Come in, my friend," said the fox. "Sit down. I am going to serve you a little something," and she brought out a flat stone which was very smooth, and spread a thin coat of atole on top of it.

"Eat with me," said the fox. The heron began to peck at the rock, but could not get anything into her mouth. The fox licked the rock clean.

Pretending to be satisfied, the heron thanked her hostess. "Tomorrow I am expecting you at my home on the seashore," said the heron.

"Good, I shall go there," answered the fox.

"Well, good bye," said the heron, and she flew away.

The next day the fox got up at dawn. By noon she arrived at her friend's house. "Come in," said the heron, "I am going to give you something." She brought out a big bottle full of oysters and said to her friend, "Let us sit down and eat together."

The fox could not reach a single oyster in the bottle. She could only lick the outside. Meanwhile, the heron put her beak into the bottle and ate all of the oysters.

When the meal was finished, the fox thanked her friend and went away. She was very ashamed.

The Cat and the Monkey

AMONG the Yaquis there was one who had as curious pets an educated cat and a very intelligent monkey. The man's name was Oname'a. He understood the language of the animals. One day the cat and the monkey were quarreling.

The monkey said to the cat, "You aren't worth anything. You don't divert the master. You don't play with him. I amuse him with my intelligence and he pets me."

The cat replied, "Well, I take care of his house. When I am about, the rats don't come into the kitchen. And those which do come never leave, because I kill them."

In the middle of this talk a rat came out of a hole and stopped near a table, wanting to get up on top of it. The cat jumped. But the rat escaped. It ran around the table and benches a few times and hid under a stone in the corner.

The monkey laughed and made fun of the cat, telling him that he was stupid and incapable.

"All right, let's see if you are any better."

The monkey went over to the corner where the rat was hidden and moved the rock. The rat ran out and up on top of the table. The monkey pursued it. The rat ran around a water jug and some pottery plates, and ran into a hole.

129

The Stories

The monkey circled all of the dishes but so stupidly that he knocked them all over with his tail, breaking them all. He didn't catch the rat, and he was very ashamed.

Then the cat said, "You think yourself more lively than I. You want to catch the rat, but you don't. Instead, you break all of the plates and the water-jug from which my master drinks. When he comes home and sees this, then you will get the punishment you deserve!"

The monkey could not answer. All he could do was bite his nails.

Señor Oname'a came in. He saw things spread all over the floor. "What went on here?" he asked.

The cat was stretched out watching the hole where the rat had disappeared.

"Well, who broke the dishes on the table?" asked Oname'a.

"I broke them," said the monkey. But he didn't lift his head.

"So you were playing around with the cat? Is that it?"

"No, Sir," said the cat, "We weren't playing. A rat came out but I couldn't catch him. Then the monkey called me stupid and incapable. So I said to him, 'You catch the rat if you think that you are better than I am.' He couldn't, but he tumbled over all the plates."

The monkey was punished for making fun of the cat. Later the rat came out and the cat gave him a blow with his left paw and killed him. He took the rat to his master who gave the rat back to the cat for his supper.

This fable is finished.

In Rabbit's House

RABBIT had a house. Into this house crawled a snake. He stayed there, waiting for the owner to return so he could eat him.

When the rabbit came home, he saw the track of the snake going into his house. So, to deceive whoever was inside, he spoke to his house, saying, "Good morning, my house."

There was no answer. A second time he greeted the house and there was no reply.

When there was no answer the third time, the rabbit said, "Oh, my house, why do you not answer me? Is something the matter?"

And again he said, "Good morning, house."

"Good morning, my patron," replied the snake from within.

Then the rabbit said, "What! Whoever heard of a house speaking? It is clear that some enemy is inside." And he went away and built himself a new house.   LC

This incident is recorded in stories collected in New Mexico, Mexico, and Chile.

Coyote and the Friendly Dogs

A COYOTE who was very hungry was walking about the outskirts of a field. He was discovered by a few dogs who were taking care of the crops. With the dogs were some little quail. This was in the time when animals talked like people and all of them understood one another.

The dogs talked to the coyote in such a way as not to frighten him, saying, "Brother, come along with us. It looks as if you are quite hungry."

"Poor little coyote," said the quail, with voices which showed their pity. "It is obvious that you are very hungry."

The coyote, thinking that they were going to give him something to eat, went with them. He walked along surrounded with dogs, for there were many dogs, and the quail followed behind him singing:

'ama mele wo'i
wo'i taka 'ama mele.

Thus the little quail sang to the coyote. But he did not like it, this song.

"Why do you sing this *'ama mele wo'i?*" the coyote asked.

"Oh, don't worry about that," said the dogs, "that is just a song." But the words of the song meant, "For the last time you are a coyote." This they sang because they were taking him off to kill him.

Before they arrived at the houses the dogs set up a great noise and barking. Men came out of the houses, but the coyote couldn't run because he was surrounded by dogs. The men took him off to where they lit a great fire, and into it they threw the poor coyote. Here ends the story.

The Black Horse

I HAD BEEN riding my black horse through the thickets of pitahaya from early morning until past midday. I had no water and the sweetness of the pitahaya honey caused me great thirst. There was no place within one hundred and sixty kilometers where I could get any water. I was getting desperate, thinking I might die any minute.

But at that moment some great, beautiful clouds formed. I looked at those clouds and jumped on my horse and rode to the top of a hill. I carried a long stick with a fork on the end of it. When I got there, I kicked my horse with my wooden spurs and he gave a great jump up toward the clouds, and I, with my forked stick, made a stab at the cloud. My aim was good. As we came down, we were followed by a torrent of fresh water.

I drank and also my horse drank and we both bathed. Water ran in all the washes. It ran deep in Sabino arroyo. From that time on there has been water in Sabino arroyo, for which we all have to thank my wonderful horse.

Duck Hunter

ONE DAY out by a lake I was duck hunting. I had a gun but I wanted to save bullets so I thought of another way to catch them. I had some string which I fastened around my waist. Then I swam under water to where the ducks were swimming above the water. I tied the ducks' legs together under water until I almost choked. By the time I had tied a great number of ducks together I burst out of the water so suddenly that all the ducks flew up, taking me with them, tangled up in the string. In a moment I was so high in the air that I could not see anything below. In order to come down, I had to shoot all the ducks, one by one, and I came down to the ground safely with my game, but disappointed because I had to use my bullets.

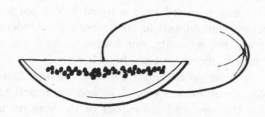

Tesak Pascola's Watermelons

WELL, GENTLEMEN, this horse of mine became very old. I let him out for a few days so that he might rest. But one day I saddled him again, to take a little turn through the monte. I traveled almost a whole day, and in the afternoon I took off the saddle. I noticed that he had a sore on his back. I turned him out. On the following day I went in search of him. I found him, lassoed him and, after cutting myself a ripe watermelon, I jumped on his back, opened the melon and rode along eating my watermelon. I came to the river and let him drink and bathed the sore on his back. I got on again and commenced eating watermelon and throwing the seeds away. Soon we came to a well and I got down. I took a little fine dirt and put it on my horse's wound, then set him free in my pasture. I went back to my house and forgot about my horse.

About four or five months later, I went in search of him. The pasture wasn't very big and didn't have much underbrush in it. It is well fenced. My horse had no means of getting out, no place to hide. Nevertheless, I could not find him. I was there an entire week without once seeing him. The following week I went in search again. One day I passed near a forest I had not seen before and stopped to contemplate the branches. It was not mesquite, nor *batamote*. As I looked, I heard a horse sneeze—brr—burr.

I went up to those branches and saw that it was a watermelon vine. I looked again and saw that the vine had grown out of the sore on my horse, aided by the dirt which I had placed on it. Some watermelon seeds had fallen into the wound.

Well, I took my horse to my house and cut many watermelons, good-sized and ripe, off of him. I sold them, and gave them to my neighbors. Later, I cut the trunk of the watermelon vine off and cured my horse.

When he died, I gave him a fiesta and did mourning for six months.

There you have it, Señores.

The Calabazas Funeral

ONE TIME I sowed lots of corn and beans and squashes, many, many squashes. When I harvested, I filled my whole house full of squashes. When I had put them all away, I fell sick. But I wasn't sick for very long, because I died. By afternoon, just about time for the sun to go down, I fell down dead.

I was alone in my house. Soon all the important people gathered to attend my funeral. Well, these great people are supposed to be served lots of food at a fiesta or a funeral and there was nothing in my house but squashes, squashes, nothing more.

They made great fires and began to cook squashes all night long. And the drum kept talking and accusing the people of eating squashes.

It said,

*kamak kamak kamak kamak kamak
kamak ka kam kamak ka kam kamak.*

This means, "sweet squashes, squashes, squashes." All night long the drum kept saying this. And it is absolutely true. Those people finished every single squash. At dawn there wasn't one squash in the house.

When they were about to bury me, I noticed that there were no more squashes, so I revived.

137

Suawaka

IN EARLIER times, there used to be serpents with seven heads. These lived northeast of Guaymas near a hill that has two little points; it is called Takalaim. Serpents with seven heads also lived in another hill, down-river and near the seashore, called So'ori.

The people of the old days say that if a Yaqui should marry a relative, he would become a serpent. He would go as a little worm into the hill, and in one year he would grow one head. By two years, he would have two heads, and at three years, he would have three. And so on, every year, he would grow a new head until he had seven. Then he would be ready to go out.

Well, when these serpents come out, they make a terrific wind and floods. Suawaka is up above watching for them. He knows that they come out every seven years, and first appears their middle head. Then Suawaka throws a harpoon of fire. This is the shooting star we see at night.

Suawaka grasps the serpent he has killed and carries it up above to his mother-in-law and father-in-law and wife. The father-in-law is Yuku, the god of thunder and lightning. Yuku's wife is the rain. They all eat this kind of serpent. Every seven years, Suawaka goes down to Takalaim, and the next seven years he goes down to So'ori. So Yuku and his family have plenty of meat. But if Suawaka doesn't come down when a serpent starts out of a hill, there is much wind and rain.

Once a man was fishing near Guaymas. He was out in a canoe when he saw Suawaka come down and kill a seven-headed serpent.

"What are you doing?" asked the fisherman.

"Killing serpents," said Suawaka.

"Where do you live?"

"Up there."

"Take me to your house," said the fisherman.

"Very well," said Suawaka. So he put the serpent meat on his shoulders, then put the fisherman to top of it.

"Close your eyes," said Suawaka. The man did, and they flew up to the other world.

The fisherman opened his eyes and saw serpent meat all around. The meat did not please him. There were scales all over it, each scale as big as a tub.

The wife of Suawaka said, "Try it. The meat is delicious." But the man could not. There was nothing else to eat up there. At last the woman said to Suawaka, "I think this man is going to die. He can't eat. I don't know why you brought him up here. It would be best to carry him down there again, Miguel." (He is really Suawaka, but sometimes he is called San Miguel.)

"Carry me back down to earth again," said the man.

"Very well. Take this serpent's scale with you so that your people can see it. Then others will not want to come up here. Close your eyes."

They went back down and arrived quickly.

The fisherman showed the Yaquis the serpent scale and all of them were frightened.

It is said that Yuku, the father-in-law of Suawaka is always very wrathful with him. When Suawaka goes down toward earth, the one-eyed Yuku throws bolts of lightning at him. This is the story. It is finished here. MT

Suawaka is described more fully in other versions of this story as a blond dwarf. The Huichol Indians also believe that shooting stars kill water monsters (Zingg 1938: 564). The Yaqui belief in a water monster associated with floods and torrential rains is also expressed by other Indians: the Aztecs, Huicholes, Cora, Mixe, and Mayos of Mexico (Parsons 1939, Vol. 2: 1009, 1016; Beals 1933: 79), and the Zuni, Hopi and Sia of the southwest (Beals 1933: 79; Parsons 1939, Vol. 2: 1003).

Topol the Clever

IN A PLACE called Sikchibei, which is situated about two kilometers from Torim toward where the sun sets, there in ancient times one of the greatest fiestas of the Yaquis took place. People from the eight pueblos attended. It was dedicated to the three divinities, Father, Son and the Holy Spirit. Nobody remained in his home.

In those times people did not know corn, beans, garbanzos, or any of these things, but the Yaquis, then, contributed roots and wild fruits. Others brought herbs to cook and give to the fiesteros to serve. Others brought deer, coyotes, and javelinas.

Here Topol performed. Topol means tiger. Here it was that he received as a reward for his cleverness a beautiful Yaqui maiden named Wotoboli Sewa Tosali.

A *kobanao* there had offered this girl to the man who could bring in, alive, without having struck it or touched it, a javelina to the fiesta. Others brought deer, lions, and dead javelina, but no one knew how to bring in a javelina he had not touched. But Topol was clever. He cut himself a stick of the wood of a plant which has blue flowers. With this stick he set out into the forest. There, he encountered a band of javelinas. All ran away but one. This one ran toward Topol. Topol did not move. He held his stick out. The javelina bit it. The animal bit the stick with great strength as if he wanted to take it away from Topol. Thus Topol began to drag on the stick and the pig didn't want to let it go. Instead, he followed wherever Topol dragged him. Pulling the stick and

141

the pig traveling behind never letting go of the stick, Topol dragged him all the way to Sikchibei, where the fiesta was taking place.

When the Indians saw Topol bring in the animal, those who were seated arose, shouting "Topol! It is he who wins Wotoboli Sewa Tosali!" All of the Indians looked with admiration at him for his great valor. Topol gave the pig to the chiefs of the fiesta. But the father of Wotoboli Sewa Tosali said to him, "There still lacks one thing before you conclude your task."

Without saying anything, Topol made as if to mount the javelina, passing over its back and pressing his legs about its ribs. This he repeated three times and it was finished.

Immediately they brought out the girl, dressed with beautiful skins and a crown of the finest bird plumes. The witnesses and god-parents appeared and the *maestros* and *cantoras*. With all of these, they appeared at the altar. There they were taken care of. Then followed the fiesta.

Later, it is said that Topol became a chief and gave battle against the Apaches. Having come out of the battle wounded by three arrows, from this he died. At his funeral great fiestas were celebrated. And it was here, for the first time, that the dance of the coyote was performed. It was sung thus:

yoli yoli yoli tamewuk yoli tamewuk
kayoli tamewukayoli tamewuk kayoli tamewuk
ponki ponki ponki pok pok pok

With this coyote song they buried the chief, Topol. And from then until today, when a soldier dies, or a Yaqui chief, in his funeral services, they sing and dance the coyote.

Why the Animals Remain Animals

BAI'IKURI was tall and very strong. He worked hard to support his children. Sometimes he would go to the sea to get fish and oysters. Other times he would go into the sierra and gather honey, roots of various kinds, and also fruit. Part of these things he would give to his children and the rest he would trade for hides in order to clothe them.

One day he came back loaded with a great deal of fruit. He was tired, and wet from sweating. He sat down on a piece of a log in the shade of a mesquite tree, rolled a cigarette, lit it, and smoked for a while.

Immediately many birds gathered around him. Among them was a bird called Wa'ikumarewi.

Sitting there in the shade, Bai'ikuri sneezed, "ha'achis!"

Wa'ikumarewi wanted to imitate him. He also sneezed, "ha'achis!" But he jerked his head so hard that his neck broke and his head flew off and fell far away.

After that none of the animals ever wanted to imitate men.

Coyote Woman

NEAR Ousekari is an arroyo called Ba'ate-bem. Here once lived a Yaqui called Mangwe Wakira, or "Manuel the Weak." Also in this place there was a little ranchería. Among those who lived there, was a Yaqui woman who enjoyed practicing the art of witchcraft. She would turn herself into a coyote. This is how she did it: she would go out into the monte, take off all of her clothes, and lie down and roll over in an ant hill. When she arose, she would be transformed into a coyote. In this form, she was referred to as Coyote Woman, or Yoem Wo'i. She was greatly feared because of her strange powers.

One cold winter dawn, Mangwe Wakira was warming himself at his fire, clothed only with some skins. He was seated with his eyes closed. He did not know it when Yoem Wo'i arrived.

She sat down across from him and said, "Awfully cold, isn't it, Mangwe?" But because of being a coyote she did not speak clearly.

When Mangwe Wakira opened his eyes and saw the naked animal close to him, forgetting both his cloak and the warm fire, he jumped up and started to run.

No one knows where Mangwe went, nor do they know if he ever returned. Here the story ends.

The First Fiesta

YOMUMULI WAS a hunter who lived near the pueblo of Juirivis. He was an old man, and he had twin sons who were called Yomumulim. The old man, walking one day through the monte, heard the beat of a drum. Although he drew near to where the drum was sounding, although he made every effort possible to find the musician, he could not see anyone.

In those days, no one yet knew about drums, nor about pascolas. So Yomumuli was hearing the first drum in the land of the Yaquis. The following day he returned to the same spot and the drummer again began to play a very pretty song. Yomumuli, who was enchanted with the music, searched again for the musician, but could not find him. He returned to his hut and chatted about this with the twins, Yomumulim.

These two boys were very obedient. Their father said to them, "Go down to that place where we rested four days ago, near a little mound of spines. There, I don't know exactly where, can be heard a beautiful thing which caused my heart to be very happy. Go then, to see if also you hear it. But don't go near those spines."

The Yomumulim twins went into the familiar monte. When they arrived at the place, the drummer was playing the most beautiful of songs. The Yomumulim listened. The drummer finished, and from beneath the pile of spines which were of

145

cholla, mesquite, and pitahaya, there appeared a
toli. This is a kind of rat which is sometimes
called *bwiya toli* because he lives underground
beneath a pile of cactus spines and thorns which
serve him as a nest.

The *toli* came out. Greeting the twins he said,
"Come into my house."

"Thank you very much, but we cannot go
in there because our father ordered us to come
this near to those spines and no nearer."

"And what more did your father tell you?"
asked the *bwiya toli*.

"Well, our father sent us here in order that
we might hear that sound in your house."

"Aha, well, this is called a drum," said the
bwiya toli, showing it to them. "And this is called
a flute," he said, showing them a carrizo flute.

"Ah, yes, thank you," said the Yomumulim.

When they arrived home they chatted with
the old man, Yomumuli, about this.

A few days later our mother Eva arrived at
the house of Yomumuli. She said to the old man,
"From this time on there shall be religious fiestas.
You, from now on, are the *moro yaut*. Your children shall make *cohetes*. Tomorrow you must
go over to see *bwiya toli* and tell him that you
are going to have a fiesta and that he should come
to play. After that, go to the Devil and have him
come to dance pascola."

Yomumuli did it all. *Bwiya toli* agreed to present himself with his drum and flute. But old
Satan said, "I shall not go to dance. Instead I
shall send my son."

Then the Devil spoke to his son. "You must
go to the fiesta and be very funny in order that

all the Yaquis may laugh. But there is one thing—
they are going to give you three *cohetes* to burn.
I do not want you to light them."

"Very well," said the little devil, and he went
to the fiesta. As soon as he arrived they gave
him three *cohetes*. "I can't light these," he said.

"And why not?" asked the fiestero.

"My father does not desire it."

"Well, you are a pascola now, and it is an
obligation of all pascolas to burn *cohetes*."

Cohetes are sacred and are burned at the hour
of prayer. By burning these, the Devil and the
other evil spirits flee far from such saintly things.
For this reason, the Devil had said to his son,
"Don't burn *cohetes*."

Well, the Devil had a desire to see his son
dance pascola, so he was there, hidden behind
some branches. When they gave the young devil
the *cohetes,* he burned one and threw it straight
at old Satan. Satan ran as fast as a bird. In the
early hours of dawn he came back, but again
they burned *cohetes* and again he had to run
away. From that time on, the Devil has not been
able to attend fiestas.

Well, this is the way Yomumuli discovered the
first drum and flute, those of the *bwiya toli* who
made the first fiesta.

Twin boy culture heroes are encountered in myth
cycles of other American tribes, such as the Zuni
(Parsons 1939, Vol. 2: 966), Hopi and Pima
(Parsons 1939, Vol. 2: 995). In a Papago myth,
twin boy heroes find the first bamboo from which
flutes were made (Densmore 1929: 61-62).

Bobok

IN ANCIENT TIMES in the Yaqui region, water became scarce for a long period of time. Yaquis were suffering from the thirst which devastated them. Water holes dried up. They made wells and couldn't find water. Rocks resembled coals of fire. All the Yaqui region was burning up from lack of water. The Indians assuaged their thirst with some half-green plants.

So, out of such necessity, they attempted to send a message to Yuku, the King of the Rain. First, they ordered up the sky sparrow. He went straight to the King of the Rain. After greeting him on behalf of the eight pueblos, the sparrow said to Yuku, "They tell me to ask you the favor of some rain."

To this the King replied, saying, "Gladly. Go without any worries. Tell your chiefs that the rain will come."

The sparrow descended with the speed of a bolt of lightning. But before he reached the Yaquis, the world became cloudy. Lightning commenced. A hurricane of wind overcame the sky sparrow. The rain, thus, never arrived at the Yaqui region.

Seeing that the sparrow did not return, the Yaquis then commanded the swallow to perform the same mission. The swallow flew up to the King of the Rain supplicating on the part of his chiefs that he send them a little water, for the Yaquis were dying of thirst.

The King answered in good humor, "Go without worry to your chiefs. After you will come the rain."

The swallow flew down, but he was also destroyed, like the sparrow, by the lightning and the wind. Neither he nor one drop of rain ever arrived at the ground.

Then the leaders of the tribe, desperate, could think of no one else to send. Until they remembered the toad. They tried to locate this toad, and finally learned where he was. He was in a place called Bahkwam, which means "lagoon" and which now is the pueblo of Bacum. There they found the toad, Bobok.

They told Bobok to come to a great council at a place near Vicam. There the principal leaders of the eight pueblos met. The toad presented himself, and they said to him, "You must go and beg rain for all of us from the King of the Rain."

"Very well," answered the toad. "With your

149

permission I will retire in order to make ready for my trip tomorrow. Wait for me and for the rain." He went off to the lagoon, Bahkwam, and visited a friend of his who was a magician and could convert himself into a bat. From him he borrowed some bats wings.

The following day Bobok flew up to the clouds and met the King of the Rain. After greeting the King and saluting him for his chiefs, Bobok said, "Sir, do not treat the Yaquis so badly. Send us a little water to drink, for we are dying of thirst."

"Very well," answered the King of the Rain. "Go ahead. Don't worry. The rain will follow you very soon."

Bobok pretended to go, but really dug into the ground at the door of the King's house. Then it clouded up, lightning was seen, thunder was heard, and it began to rain. In fact, the rain almost reached the earth. But it could not find Bobok. It stopped, and began to run along on top of the wind. Then Bobok ran along on top of the rain, saying *"Kowak, kowak, kowak."*

The rain, hearing the toad, began to fall again. The toad stopped singing. The rain, thinking toad was dead, again became calm. So Bobok began singing and moving over the top of the rain toward the earth. At last the rain struck the Yaqui region, still searching for the toad in order to kill him.

It rained all over the earth, and suddenly there were many toads, all singing. Bobok returned the bat wings to his magician friend and lived on peacefully in his lagoon, Bahkwam.

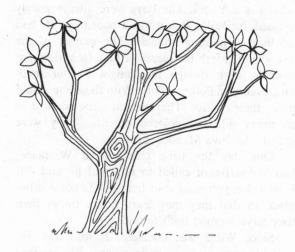

The Five Mended Brothers

IN THE SIERRA of Toma'arisi there lived a Yaqui named Wiloa Bakot. This sierra, both high and low and all about it, was populated by people. Of them, many thousands were Yaquis. Quite a number of Yaquis lived also in the nearby hills. Their chief was called Baka Wecheme. He was a good man. He loved his people and desired that they should love good and useful things.

Well, it happened that Wiloa Bakot fell in with a little Yaqui woman who was quite pretty and who was named Gi'iku'ure Sewa. When these two were married there was a great reunion and

151

the fiestas of the marriage lasted for eight days. Afterwards they lived very tranquilly. They had five children, all boys.

When the boys were of an age to study, the parents put them in the hands of a wise priest who was a Yaqui. The boys were always poorly dressed, for Wiloa Bakot was a poor man. He had no luck at hunting animals. The mother of the five would search for pieces of hide from different animals, even though they might be but small bits, even of different colors. With these she would make their clothes. They looked quite comical in so many different colored patches. They were called The Five Mended Brothers.

One day the tribe chief, Baka Wecheme, had Wiloa Bakot called to him and he said, "It is well that you send your five sons to some other place so that they may learn better things than they have learned until today."

Since Wiloa was obedient, he did this. He told his sons to leave their village. The mother fixed them a lunch.

With this little food, the five mended ones took to the road in the direction of the setting sun. They traveled all day, from early morning until late. At dusk they descended into a deep canyon, steep sided with high hills bordering it. This canyon was very dark and dangerous because of the presence of brave animals like tigers and wolves. Also there were serpents which were large and venomous. In this arroyo they traveled in the dark.

Now they came upon a place where there was water, and a large tree with many branches above. There they ate. And when they had lain down, the oldest brother said to them all, "Brothers, here under this tree we will meet again in order to return, all together, to our home, within a year. He who gets here first must wait for the others."

"Very well," they all said, and they slept until morning. The following day, after eating some roots for nourishment, they traveled on out of the canyon with care because of the great danger from wild beasts and serpents.

On coming out of the canyon they entered upon a great mesa without vegetation of any sort. It was completely arid and contained no plants, nor animals to hunt. On this mesa there was nothing to eat, nothing to drink.

After much travel over that shadeless plain with no where to stop and rest, they came upon a place where five trails parted. One was in the center, going straight toward the sunset. Two went off to the right and two to the left.

There the five brothers stopped, the five thirsty, mended, torn Yaqui boys and the oldest of them said, "Here are five roads and we are five. I will take the center road and you each choose yours. In a year we shall unite again beneath that tree. He who gets there first will wait for the others."

They all bid one another good-bye and each took his own road.

The older brother arrived at a pueblo, a very beautiful town, very fertile. In this pueblo he studied to become a magician.

The second boy came to a hill where people worked with wood. Here they made bows and arrows better than in another place.

Successively, each boy arrived at the place for which he was destined. They put themselves in the hands of intelligent men and studied with great effort throughout the year. At the end of the year, one after the other, they returned to the big tree they had designated as their place of reunion.

When they were all there under the tree, the elder brother questioned them about what they had learned.

"I am a good carpenter," said the first.

"I am good at shooting," said the second.

"I am good at reviving the dead," said the third brother.

"I am a good thief," said the fourth.

"I know how to prophecy wisely," said the elder. "Right now, above us in this tree is a crow sleeping in her nest and she has three eggs. I want you, good thief, to climb up and rob her of an egg without awakening her."

"Very well," said the thief. And he commenced to ascend the tree. He came to the nest, put his hand under the bird, and robbed an egg which he took down to his brother.

And the elder brother said to the carpenter, "Let me see you make an egg exactly like this real one."

"Very well," said the carpenter. Taking a little piece of wood, he made an egg and handed it to his elder brother, who broke the real egg.

The elder brother handed the wooden egg to the crafty thief and said, "Climb up and put this egg into the nest. Then frighten the bird."

The thief climbed up and put the egg in the nest and frightened the bird, who flew out.

"Let's see you, good shot, knock down that bird," said the elder brother.

Good shot took his bow and shot. The bird fell down dead.

"Let me see you, he who revives the dead, bring that bird back to life."

The young magician immediately cured the bird and it flew away.

Thus all were satisfied in seeing the manifestations of their various arts and they slept until the following morning. Again they took to the road in the direction of their home where they were received by their parents.

Their father, Wiloa Bakot, went to visit Baka Wecheme, the chief, and said, "My sons have now returned, all of them very intelligent. The eldest is a diviner."

"Send him to me immediately," said Baka Wecheme. Wiloa Bakot ordered his wise son to go to the chief, and when he arrived the chief said to him, "Yesterday I lost my wife's gold watch. Tell me where it is."

"Here it is, Sir. You, yourself, put it here in order to see if I were a diviner or not." And he found it in the chief's house.

The chief was very contented and gave some pieces of gold and silver to the boy. "The brother after you, what does he know how to do?" asked the chief.

"He is very good at shooting the bow. There is no one who can better him."

"Good. Send him to me," said Baka Wecheme. When the marksman presented himself, the chief set up a bird's feather on a tree twenty-five paces away.

Good shot took his bow, and with an arrow knocked over the feather. The chief was very contented. He gave the boy a suit made of tiger skin. "And now your next brother, what does he know how to do?"

"That one knows how to revive the dead."

"Well, send him to me."

Then Baka Wecheme killed a little son of his. The magician brother arrived and gave the boy life again, and the chief was contented. "Now send me the next brother and we will see what he knows how to do."

"He is a good carpenter."

This one presented himself and quickly made many bows, a violin, and a mouth bow. And he received as a reward a beautiful headdress of colored feathers.

"Now send me your little brother. Let us see what he can do."

"Oh, that one can't come. His work is evil."

"Well, it is all work," said Baka Wecheme.

The father did not want his youngest son to go to the chief. So he himself went to Baka Wecheme and said, "Respected sir, I do not desire that my youngest son come here because he is a thief and I am afraid that you might feel the need to kill him."

"Have no fear. Tell your boy that tonight I am going to place five beautiful suits of hide in a place far away from here, also a good deal of gold and silver. Twenty-five soldiers will guard this. If the boy is crafty at robbing, he will go there and steal it, and it will be for him."

"Very well," said Wiloa Bakot. And he went to advise his son.

The thief mixed a little narcotic in some wine and put it in an olla, which he took with him. Then he went off to where the Yaqui soldiers were guarding the treasure. As he approached them, he began to shout.

"I am lost!" he repeated many times.

At last the captain of the twenty-five said, "Go you, and find who is lost and bring him here." They went and found him.

"Where do you come from?" they asked the young man.

"From Chunakotia and I am on my way to Tetamolaim."

"Sleep here tonight, and tomorrow you may go on your way."

"Very well," said the thief. He took a swallow of wine and said to the soldiers, "Have some wine to make your vigil more enjoyable."

All of them had some wine. They fell asleep, and the thief took the clothes and the gold and silver and went away.

On the following day the father, Wiloa Bakot, presented himself to the respected Baka Wecheme and said, "My youngest son has done what you asked him to do."

"My soldiers told me," said the chief. "It is well. Here is the reward." And he sent the thief a gift. "Now tell your son that he should leave this place. I don't want him here in Toma'arisi. He should go to some other place."

"Very well," said Wiloa Bakot. And he told his son he should leave for some other part.

The thief went away. Wiloa Bakot and his other sons remained there with much respect until they died of old age.

The First Fire

NOW THERE IS fire in all rocks, in all sticks. But long ago there wasn't any fire in the world, and all of the Yaquis and the animals and the creatures of the sea, everything that lived, gathered in a great council in order to understand why there was no fire.

They knew that somewhere there must be fire, perhaps in the sea, maybe on some islands, or on the other side of the sea. For this reason, Bobok, the Toad, offered to go get this fire. The Crow offered to help him and also the Roadrunner and the Dog. These four, the winged animals and the dog, went along to help. But Bobok, the Toad, alone, knew how to enter the water of the sea and not die.

The God of Fire would not permit anyone to take his fire away. For this reason he still sends thunderbolts and lightning at anyone who carries light or fire. He is always killing them.

But Bobok entered the house of the God of Fire and stole the fire. He carried it in his mouth, traveling through the waters. Lightning and thunder made a great noise and many flashes. But Bobok came on, safe beneath the waters. Then there formed on the flooding water, little whirlpools of water full of rubbish and driftwood.

Suddenly not only one toad was to be seen, but many swam in the waters, many, many toads. They were all singing and carrying little bits of fire. Bobok had met his sons and had given some fire to one, then another, until every toad had some. These carried fire to the land where they were awaited by the Dog, the Roadrunner, and the Crow. Bobok gave his fire to those who could not enter the water.

The God of Fire saw this and threw lightning at the Crow and the Roadrunner and the Dog. But many toads kept on coming and bearing fire to the world. These animals gave light to all the things in the world. They put it into sticks and rocks. Now men can make fire with a drill because the sticks have fire in them. LC

The Spirit Fox

AN INDIAN lived in the region of the hill
west of Bacum. This man's name was Ba'ayoeria.
Alone, he and his woman lived. They had neighbors a little distance away to the north, and others
farther away to the south. Ba'ayoeria was not a
hunter. He lived from collecting roots for medicines and edible roots. Also he collected blossoms
from trees for use in tanning hides and others for
medicines. He would load them in some coyote
or fox hide sacks, or wildcat skin sacks. Then he
would set out, carrying various sacks full of roots
and flowers, crossing the hills and higher mountains to the edge of the sea. All these things he
would exchange for dried fish, clams, oysters, and
salt—all of these for his woman, and for his
neighbors who brought him skins in exchange for
salt, fish and oysters. In this way, he was living.

One day when Ba'ayoeria traveled in search of roots, a fox passed in front of him and stopped, gazing at him. Ba'ayoeria went on his way, looking back now and again at the fox who was still watching him.

The same thing happened the second day. On the third day, at the same place, the fox came out and spoke, saying, "Listen to me, Ba'ayoeria. This is a true thing. I am your friend. I am not really a fox, but I asked permission to come here with you because I am looking at a great danger that will come to you and I want to save you. This night an individual is coming with intentions to kill you. Your woman is having amorous relations with this man and they are agreed upon killing you. For some time they have been playing treasonously with you. Tonight don't lie down in your bed in the place where you are accustomed to sleep. Put your wife there where you usually sleep because she has told the man, 'Thus you may kill him as he sleeps and we will live together without danger from Ba'ayoeria.' Thus your wife spoke."

All of this, the fox told to Ba'ayoeria who then asked, "Who are you?"

"I am the soul of that lost body you buried near Buram Teopo. In gratitude for your having buried my body, I, today, advise you."

"Good, then, little fox," said the Indian.

The fox disappeared into the thicket and the man returned to his hut, and to his woman. That evening, after supper they chatted awhile. The two appeared to be contented, nothing could be seen, not a bad word or a bad look. The two conversed until bedtime came.

161

And when it came time to lie down, the man said to the wife, "Let us change places. You sleep in my place, and I in yours."

The woman took her head in her hands, and he asked, "Why do you appear so sad?"

"I don't know what happened to me," replied the woman.

"Come, then, lie down in my place and you will feel better," he said. The woman lay down and pretended to sleep.

But Ba'ayoeria did not sleep. Late at night the traitor came quietly. He moved up to the bed where the woman lay, thinking it was Ba'ayoeria. He lifted his arm and gave a great stab with his sharp, wooden lance. Ba'ayoeria arose, threw himself on the man and overcame him. He tied him firmly with ropes and waited for the dawn to come. In the morning he buried his woman.

He took the assassin to Bacum. There, the man was punished with lashes until blood gushed from between his shoulder-blades. From these lashes he died two days later.

Ba'ayoeria married another young girl, and continued his work of trading roots and flowers.

The Yaqui Doctor

AN OLD Yaqui man had twelve sons. When the thirteenth son came along, no one in the village wanted to take him as a god-son. Thirteen sons was just one too many.

The father became angry. "I go now," he said. "I don't care for this pueblo." He went off in the direction of the mountains. "Out here among the animals, the first one I meet, he shall be my *compadre.*"

A man came toward him. He was tall and distinguished looking. "Where do you go?" he asked the father of thirteen sons.

"Anywhere."

"You go in search of someone who would serve as your *compadre?*"

"How did you know?"

"I am the Devil."

"I am a poor man," said the father. "You are for the rich. Go away."

The Devil went away in a great yellow cloud of reeking dust.

163

Then a second man appeared. He was tall, slender, and respectable looking. He had a sword. He said to the father, "Where are you going, good man?"

"I go in search of someone who would serve me as *compadre*."

"I will serve you. And I will promise that when your son grows up he will be a doctor, a good doctor, the best."

"Who are you?"

"I am Death."

"Well, since you take all from rich and poor alike, good. You will be my *compadre*."

"When you enter the church I will be there," said Death. "Bring your son."

The old man returned to his pueblo. His son was baptized.

When the boy was thirteen years old, his father again met Death who said, "I told you this boy is going to be a good doctor. Leave him to me for instruction."

Since that was the agreement, Death carried the boy away. They entered a hill, into a huge room. There were six other rooms, all very big. In each room there were different flowers, and many candles burning. These were the lives of Yaqui men. "This herb is used for a certain sickness," Death said. "This also is a cure."

Thus, he taught the boy. "Each time you visit a sick man, I will be there. When you see my form at the head of a sick man you will cure him. But when you see me at the foot of the sick man, know then that he must die and give him no medicine."

The boy went out to cure, and always he was a good doctor. Word went out that he was good at curing. He always asked a great deal of money, so by the time he was thirty years old, he was very rich. People came to him from all over. And always, he did as his god-father had advised.

Finally a King who was very sick called him and said that whoever made him well could marry his daughter. The doctor thought very much of the King's daughter and she begged him to make her father well.

When he saw Death standing at the King's feet, he quickly turned the King about, and administered the medicine.

The King got well and the princess was very happy. "Let us go to the church," she said.

After the marriage, Death was standing at the door of the church. To his god-son he said, "You got yourself married, I see."

"Yes," replied the young doctor.

"Come with me," said Death, and they went to another hill. Inside were candles, some of them just beginning to burn, others half gone, others lying about extinguished on the ground. The boy begged to be shown his own candle. "This is your candle," said Death.

And he blew it out. LC

The Twins

THESE TWINS were born near the hill of Huri Kawi, near here and not very far from the railroad track.

Their mother was called Hekka Nibino. She died when they were born. The grandparents brought them up. One twin they named Cho'i and after a time he learned to be a cowboy. He came out very well.

The other twin came out a thief. He liked very much to rob. He appeared to be a natural magician. He stole and no one saw him. For this reason they called him Hi'ikia.

Thus the two grew up and when they were finally men, Cho'i had the luck of marrying a fairly pretty Yaqui girl. She owned a great many goats, horses, and cows; in fact, it was a very pretty ranch where the two lived.

Hi'ikia went on with his profession of robbing. But the wife of Cho'i was not acquainted with her husband's twin brother. One day Cho'i talked to his woman, telling her, "I have a brother who looks very much like me. Don't get us confused. This brother of mine enjoys very much to steal. I warn you carefully. If he should come here when I'm not about, do me the favor of escorting him through every part of the house so he may see all that is here. That which you do not show him he will steal. So it is necessary that he see everything, that he might rob us of nothing."

"It is well," answered the woman. Cho'i saddled up his horse to go out and see his cattle. It was late when he went off.

After a time, Hi'ikia came up and saluted the woman. She looked, and looked again; she talked to him, and believed him to be her husband. His face was the same as that of her man, his mode of speech and the build of his body. She was very confused.

Finally she said, "Come, in order that you may see my house." And she took him where she kept her treasure. She let him see everything except some cheeses. Hi'ikia stayed until evening, and they ate supper. They were eating their supper when Cho'i returned and greeted his brother.

After supper, they went to bed. Later in the night, Cho'i said, "I am going now. I'll be back in a little while. I am going to look for some cattle on the other side of the river."

When Cho'i left, Hi'ikia entered the storehouse, took a cheese and went away. Just outside he stepped on a thorn and cried, "Ay, ay, ay! I pricked myself!"

The woman thought it was her husband whom she heard cry and she got up to see about it. Hi'ikia quickly pulled out the thorn and went on his way with the cheese.

The wife looked all around. Finally her husband returned and she said to him, "Tell me what happened?"

"Nothing. All went well," replied Cho'i. He took her by the hand and they went back to their room to bed. After a while, he asked her, "Why did you ask me what happened?"

"Because you cried out, 'Ay, I pricked myself!'"

"But, I didn't."

"I heard your voice."

"Ah, well. It was my brother, Hi'ikia. Tell me. How many things did you show him?"

"I showed him everything, the treasure, the arms, the corral, the calves—Oh!" said the woman, "that one thing which I didn't show him were the cheeses."

"And how many cheeses did you have?"

"Eight," she said.

"Come, let us look," said Cho'i, and they looked, and there were only seven cheeses. "One cheese my brother carried off," Cho'i said, "I am going to take it from him." And he left.

Cho'i knew where his brother was hidden. He went straight there. Hi'ikia had left the cheese with a friend, saying, "Take care of this cheese. I am going to steal some corn to eat with it. I'll be back soon." And he went off.

Before approaching the camp, Cho'i cried out, "Ay, I pricked myself!"

The man guarding the cheese thought that it was Hi'ikia and he said, "I will help you!"

But Cho'i said, "No, don't come. I go now. Better that you should gather up some fire-wood."

"Good," said the Yaqui with the cheese,

Leaving the cheese, he went off to gather wood.

Cho'i took the stolen cheese and returned with it to his house.

When Hi'ikia came back with many ears of corn, he asked his friend about the cheese. He didn't see it where it had been left. His friend did not know where it was.

"Who has been here?" asked Hi'ikia.

"Nobody has been here."

"Then why did you go to gather wood?"

"Because you told me to."

"Aha, tell me, how was that?"

"You said, 'Ay, I have pricked myself!' and I said, 'Wait, and I will come and help you,' but you said to go on out and gather wood so I left the cheese and went to gather firewood."

"Aha," said Hi'ikia. "That was my brother."

They roasted the ears in the coals and ate only corn. Then they went to sleep.

All this took place that night. The next day they got up to go in search of food in other parts. Hi'ikia did not return again to his brother's house, and Cho'i lived tranquilly with his wife, taking care of his cattle.

Hi'ikia continued to rob in order to eat. Thus each one proceeded at his own profession until, together, on the same day, they died.

It is likely that there once existed more complete legends about the twin Yaqui boy culture heroes (Fabila 1940: 238), since other tribes have longer stories about similar characters. The Papagos have a myth wherein such twins find the first bamboo for the making of the flute (Densmore 1929: 61-62). Stories about twins with unusual powers are found in the mythology of the Navajos, the Pimas, Hopis (Parsons 1939, Vol. 2: 995) and Zunis (Benedict 1935: 264-265). Other isolated incidents in Yaqui mythology seem to connect it with that of other American aborigines and suggest the kinds of stories which may have been lost through acculturation. The story of "Suawaka" and the myth "When Badger Named the Sun," have affiliations with parts of the elaborate, pagan myth cycle of the Huicholes of Mexico in which falling stars are said to kill the rain serpents of Nakwe (Zingg 1938: 564) and in which a gathering is said to have been held for the purpose of naming the sun (Zingg 1938: 517). Also, as in Yaqui mythology, measuring land is important in Huichol stories, and the wind is considered evil as it is in the Yaqui myth, "Yuku." The myth of a cannibal bird monster is found in the stories of the Cochiti (Benedict 1931: 211), Pima and Papago Indians (Densmore 1929: 45-54).

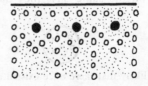

The Snake
of the Hill of Nohme

IN A LARGE waterhole under the hill of Nohme there lives a big snake with a cross on its forehead. This monster lives on water animals but sometimes it eats cattle, goats, and even people. It makes a great wind with its indrawn breath and sucks them right into its mouth. This snake's name is Acencio. He was once a *maestro* in the church.

But this *maestro* did evil things. When he died and they buried him, at once the grave began to sink. The sky became cloudy and dark and from the hole where the grave had been was heard a noise such as a lion makes.

Then a priest came who knew how to talk Yaqui, and said, "Go, Acencio, go to a place where there are no Christians."

At once the animal began to break the earth and travel below the surface of the ground. Many people walked behind the moving mound, praying, so that the monster might not remain in the pueblo. The priest also followed along, praying, until at last the snake reached the foot of the hill of Nohme. Breaking the rock, he went deep under the hill into the water which is inside of that hill. There, it is said, Acencio still lives.

A similar monster is described in the myths of the Papago, the Pueblos (Parsons 1939, Vol. 2: 1003; Benedict 1935: 326), and the Cora (Beals 1933: 79).

171

The Stories

Tukawiru

WE KNOW that all animals have a father, or a leader of their kind, the eagles, buzzards, all. The chief of the Buzzards is called Tukawiru, or Night Buzzard. No one knows where Tukawiru lives, not even the birds themselves.

It happened that a young man entered into a game with a gambler, a devil, or maybe just someone employed by the Devil. This gambler won all of the young man's money. Then he won the boy's clothes.

When all was lost, the gambler said, "I will stake a thousand pesos against your heart, but not now. You must come to my home."

"Where do you live?"

"At the House of the Wind."

Then the gambler asked all the animals that fly in the air to come to him, and they tried to find him, day and night, and he said to the young man, "They are searching for me. I will now take you to the House of the Wind. It is a dangerous journey. You must carry in your hand some pieces of liver. We will travel through three different winds. Each time we enter one of these winds you must shout 'Hesuta 'achai' (Jesus, Father) and put a piece of liver into my mouth."

The young man climbed on the back of Tukawiru (for that is who it was) and closed his eyes, as directed. They flew fast, very fast. The first dangerous wind they entered was very bitter. The young man fed the giant bird a piece of liver. The second wind they encountered was stinking. They passed through it in the same manner and encountered the third and most terrible wind which was very thick.

Thus, from midnight to dawn the young man rode on the back of Tukawiru. After shouting "Hesuta 'achai" three times and feeding him as many times, they arrived. The Devil stopped. He was two hundred feet from a tall tree. There the young man saw a white house which is the House of the Wind. He who lived there was not the Wind, but was he who commands the Wind.

Tukawiru said, "My friend, come into the house. Go to the kitchen and my daughter will give you something to eat."

This daughter of the Devil was not evil as were her sisters and parents. Because of this, her father forced her to be his cook and housemaid. She received the young man well, liking him more than she liked her father.

The Devil cared little for this daughter because she did good things. He had others whom he dearly loved for their bad intentions.

All was in favor of the young man because Jesucristo was watching over him. The Devil wanted to kill him, but he could not.

So the sun rose to go to work, for we all must work, and the Devil said to the young man, "Today you are to sow this land." And he pointed to some twenty acres.

It was a great deal of work to sow that much land, and he had no helpers.

But the girl said to the young man, "I will help you." She showed him a hoe, saying "Take this hoe to the field and say to it 'Sow.'"

The young man did this and the hoe worked all day, finishing at sundown.

The next day the Devil told the young man to go out and harvest the wheat which he had sown, for it was already ripe.

Again the Devil's daughter advised the young man, and the wheat was harvested.

Another day the Devil pointed out a great pile of firewood lying some distance from the house. "Cut that wood," he ordered.

The girl gave the young man an axe, and the wood was cut. But the Devil began to suspect his daughter. The next day he said to the young man, "Now you are going to build a temple, like those used by Priests. I want to go to Mass."

So the young man and the Devil's daughter and Jesucristo made a very proper temple.

Then the girl said to the boy, "I wish to take you away now. Let us leave this night." This girl was called Tosalisewa, meaning White Flower.

Each night her mother and father were accustomed to calling to her every hour in order to know if she were still there. She would always reply, "I am here." This evening her father called out and there was no reply.

The two lovers were now far away. They

had crossed the three winds by shouting "Hesuta 'achai." They arrived at the seashore. There White Flower had a boat hidden in the tules.

Meanwhile, the Devil pursued them, playing the game called *womi* in order to travel very fast, kicking a round ball ahead of him.

When the Devil arrived at the seashore, he made a boat. At last he caught the two. But the girl made the boy turn into a tadpole and she became a water plant which moves gently and plays under the water. When the Devil could not find them, he returned to his house. So White Flower's mother said that she, herself, would go after them. And so she did.

Tukawiru's wife was even more powerful than her husband. As she pursued them she played *ochia bweha*. This is an old Yaqui game played by the women. A wooden ball is thrown with a long basket, and chased, as in running the *womi*. She caught up with the boy and girl as they entered the beginning of the Yaqui land. She could follow them no farther. Then this evil mother cursed Tosalisewa saying that White Flower would love the young man but that he would not care for her.

And it was so. In Guaymas the boy joined his real wife, and he forgot all about Tosalisewa, completely. Here it ends. There is no more. LC

Cho'oko Baso

NEAR the hill of Maatale lived a Yaqui named Cho'oko Baso who worked at collecting bark from trees with which to make dyes and to tan hides. The hides he sold for fruit and roots with which to feed his sons.

One day he was walking over a stretch of coarse sand and, on passing close to a cliff very late in the evening, he saw in the middle of the cliff a white light. But he saw no windows or doors. He was standing there for some time when suddenly there appeared before him an elderly man in a long shirt, a sort of tunic, and the man asked him, "What do you search for?"

Cho'oko Baso replied, "I walk here in search of woods for use in tanning hides."

"But look," said the old man, "don't work so hard. Take this little stick and touch that rock."

Cho'oko Baso did so, and the rock opened before him: A beautiful girl appeared and said to him, "Take this little stick. When you find yourself in need, tell it to give food to your sons. Say, 'Give me money' and it will be given to you."

This is what Cho'oko Baso did. And from then on he was very rich.

But it is said that after some twenty years, Cho'oko Baso was passing by that same place and to him appeared the same old man. And the old man told him to go over to that same rock. "Touch that rock with the stick," the old man said as before.

And Cho'oko Baso did this. And the young woman appeared as before and said, "Come in."

Cho'oko Baso went inside the rock to remain there enchanted, forever.

Now when Yaquis pass by that place they turn their heads away.

References

BEALS, RALPH

    1932a   The Comparative Ethnology of Northern Mexico before 1750. *Ibero-Americana:* 2. University of California Press, Berkeley.

    1932b   Aboriginal Survivals in Mayo Culture. *American Anthropologist,* Vol. 34, No. 1, pp. 28–39. Menasha.

    1933   Modern Serpent Beliefs in Mexico. *Mexican Folkways*, Vol. 8, No. 2, pp. 77–82. Mexico.

BENEDICT, RUTH

    1931   Tales of the Cochiti Indians. *Bureau of American Ethnology, Bulletin* 98. Washington.

    1935   *Zuni Mythology*, Vol. 2. Columbia University Press, New York.

BOAS, FRANZ

    1912   Notes on Mexican Folk-Lore. *Journal of American Folk-Lore*, Vol. 25, pp. 204–260. New York.

    1941   *Nociones de Historia del Estado de Sonora.* Imprenta Cruz Galvez, Hermosillo.

CHESKY, JANE

    Field Notes.

DECORME, GERARD

    1941   *La Obra de los Jesuítas Mexicanos Durante la Epoca Colonial — 1572–1767.* Antigua Librería Robredo de José Porrúa e Hijos, Mexico.

DENSMORE, FRANCES

    1929   Papago Music. *Bureau of American Ethnology, Bulletin* 90. Washington.

    1932   Yuman and Yaqui Music. *Bureau of American Ethnology, Bulletin* 110. Washington.

177

DOMINGUEZ, F. A.

    1937a   Costumbres Yaquis. *Mexican Folkways,* Yaqui Number, July, pp. 6–24. Mexico.

    1937b   Música Yaqui. *Mexican Folkways,* Yaqui Number, July, pp. 32–44. Mexico.

ESPINOSA, A. M.

    1911   New Mexican-Spanish Folk-Lore: Folk Tales. *Journal of American Folk-Lore,* Vol. 24, pp. 397–444. American Folk-Lore Society, Lancaster.

    1914a   New Mexican-Spanish Folk-Lore. *Journal of American Folk-Lore,* Vol. 27, pp. 105–147. American Folk-Lore Society, Lancaster.

    1914b   Comparative Notes on New Mexican and Mexican Spanish Folk-Tales. *Journal of American Folk-Lore,* Vol. 27, pp. 211–231. American Folk-Lore Society, Lancaster.

FABILA, ALFONSO

    1940   *Las Tribus Yaquis de Sonora, su Cultura y Anhelada Autodeterminación.* Departmento de Asuntos Indígenas. Mexico.

GAMIO, MANUEL

    1937   La Importancia del Folk-Lore Yaqui. *Mexican Folkways,* July, pp. 45–51. Mexico.

HERNANDEZ, FORTUNANTO

    1902   *Las Razas Indígenas de Sonora y la Guerra del Yaqui.* Casa Editorial J. de Elizalde, Mexico.

HOLDEN, W. C., AND OTHERS

    1936   Studies of the Yaqui Indians of Sonora, Mexico. *Texas Technological College Bulletin,* Vol. 12, No. 1, *Scientific Series,* No. 2. Lubbock.

JOHNSON, J. B.

    1940   Diccionario Yaqui-Español. MS, Department of Anthropology, University of Arizona.

KROEBER, A. L.
  1934   Uto-Aztecan Languages of Mexico. *Ibero-Americana:* 8. University of California Press, Berkeley.

LINTON, R. L.
  1936   *The Study of Man.* D. Appleton-Century, New York.

MALINOWSKI, BRONISLAW
  1926   *Myth in Primitive Psychology.* W. W. Norton and Company, New York.

MASON, J. A. AND A. M. ESPINOSA (EDITORS)
  1914   Folk-Tales of the Tepecanos. *Journal of American Folk-Lore,* Vol. 27, pp. 148–211. American Folk-Lore Society, Lancaster.

PARSONS, E. C.
  1939   *Pueblo Indian Religion.* 2 vols. University of Chicago Publications in Anthropology, Ethnological Series. University of Chicago Press, Chicago.

SAUER, CARL
  1934   The Distribution of Aboriginal Tribes and Languages in Northwestern Mexico. *Ibero-Americana:* 5. University of California Press, Berkeley.

SPICER, E. H.
  1940a   The Yaqui Indians of Arizona. *Kiva,* Vol. 5, No. 6, pp. 21–24. Tucson.
  1940b   *Pascua, a Yaqui Village in Arizona.* University of Chicago Publications in Anthropology. University of Chicago Press, Chicago.
  1943a   The Yaqui: Sonora's Fighting Farmers. *Arizona Highways,* Vol. 14, No. 1. Phoenix.
  1943b   Linguistic Aspects of Yaqui Acculturation. *American Anthropologist,* Vol. 45, No. 3, pp. 410–434. Menasha.

SPICER, E. H. AND R. B.

    1942   Field Notes. On file at Department of Anthropology, University of Arizona, Tucson.

SPICER, R. B.

    1939   The Easter Fiesta of the Yaqui Indians of Pascua, Arizona. MS, University of Chicago.

TOOR, FRANCES

    1937a   The Yaqui Festival Makers. *Mexican Folkways,* Yaqui Number, July, pp. 26–32. Mexico.

    1937b   Notes on Yaqui Customs. *Mexican Folkways,* Yaqui Number, July, pp. 52–64. Mexico.

TRONCOSO, F. P.

    1905   *Las Guerras con las Tribus Yaquis y Mayos del Estado de Sonora.* Departmento de Estado Mayor, Mexico.

WILDER, C. S.

    1940   The Yaqui Deer Dance: A Study in Cultural Change. MS, master's thesis, University of Arizona, Tucson.

ZINGG, R. M.

    1938   *The Huichols: Primitive Artists.* Contributions to Ethnography, Vol. 1. University of Denver.